A Bottle in the Cupboard

WOMEN AND ALCOHOL

DISCARD

First Published in Ireland in 1993 by
Attic Press
4 Upper Mount Street
Dublin 2

British Library Cataloguing in Publication Data

Ward, Yvonne
    Bottle in the Cupboard: Women and Alcohol
    I. Title
    362.29

ISBN 1-855940-663

HV
S 137
. W37
1993
cop. 1

The right of Yvonne Ward to be identified as the author of this work is asserted in accordance with the Copyright, Designs and Patents Act 1988.

Cover Design: Judith O'Dwyer
Origination: Sinéad Bevan, Attic Press
Printing: Guernsey Press Ltd.

Dedication

This book is dedicated to all those women and men who have shared their suffering due to alcohol dependency with me over the last number of years.

I salute their courage and honesty and thank them for the privilege of working with them.

Acknowledgements

The author would like to acknowledge all those who have made this book possible: God; my parents; the staff (past and present) and clients of the Rutland Centre; Helena Roche who thought I could do it; Gráinne Healy my patient editor who kept my nose to the grindstone; Maeve Kneafsey for her encouragement and all the staff of Attic Press, Grace and Sharon my willing and efficent typists; Agnes Dunne-Fox my sometime courier and friend; Rosleen Thompson and Eoin Stephens for their support and encouragement, all my many other friends; and not least the fellowship of Alcoholics Anonymous.

The publishers would like to acknowledge Tipperary Water for their sponsorship and support in this book.

About the author

Yvonne Ward is a psychologist and senior counsellor with *The Rutland Centre*. She has spent the last decade actively involved in working with individuals and families affected by addiction. Yvonne currently lives and works in Dublin.

Contents

Preface

This book has as its goal the description and clarification, in everyday, ordinary language, of alcohol dependency and how it affects and imprisons those individuals suffering from it. Over the years while working with alcoholics, drug addicts and compulsive gamblers I have constantly been impressed with the intelligence, sensitivity and high level of dedication, insight and care shown by those individuals who recovered from this illness. This has highlighted for me the destructive and all encompassing distortion of the mind, body and spirit that occurs when they become addicted to alcohol and/or any other mood-altering chemical or substance.

Side by side with this awareness is the realisation that most people have little understanding or insight into the true nature and complexity of this illness which affects so many individuals and their families. This ignorance and lack of clear information on the subject has added to the chronic suffering of these people and their families.

Alcohol is still perceived by many as the guaranteed friend. Its effect, its reassuring comfort and relief is dependable, constant and relatively cheap. There are no hidden agendas, no strings attached, or so it is believed by those who return again and again to the warmth of alcohol's embrace. And so, innocently, begins the relationship which for some women becomes the most important, the most compulsive, the most overwhelming and demanding relationship in their life.

Censure, intolerance and misunderstanding of the nature of alcohol dependency means that even today alcoholic women are often perceived as immoral, perverted, unnatural and hard-hearted. Prejudice and stigma still surrounds those women who have become addicted to alcohol making their shame more intense and their denial of their illness more rigid and more difficult to remove. These women are ill, out of control, and unable to stop drinking without support. The simple steps towards intervention which can make possible her realisation of her illness and trigger her desire to recover are often unknown. Frequently friends and family wait for her to stop or to change, not realising how powerless she is or the fact that this illness is progressive and chronic and will neither get better nor stop without intervention and further support.

When approached by Attic Press to write this book I welcomed the opportunity to chronicle the seriousness and totality of an illness which is a blameless disease. No woman sets out to become an alcoholic. No woman intentionally destroys herself and her family by drinking. Hopefully this book will help those who read it to understand the seriousness of an illness which overwhelms and engulfs the lives of those women who suffer from it.

The unmanageability of the lives of those women who are alcohol dependant is illustrated here by the stories of three women. They are entirely fictional and are not based on any individual. These characters are rather the conglomeration of many women. The possibility and hope of recovery is an important aspect of any book on alcohol dependency. I offer all those who read this book my prayerful encouragement as they start on the path to recovery.

Yvonne Ward
April 1993

Chapter One
The beginnings of alcoholism

Three precious lives

It was late evening and she had had a long hard day. With a thankful sigh Susan shut the bedroom door on her sleeping child and proceeded down the stairs with her armful of dirty clothes. Just the washing to put on, the vegetables to prepare and the lunches to make for tomorrow, then I can relax, she thought. Ed wasn't home yet; the company had sent him down the country for the day.

As Susan filled the sink with water, she filled her mug from the bottle of vodka which she kept behind the bleach, detergents and fabric softeners on the top shelf of the overhead cupboard. She kept it safe there, where the children couldn't reach it, away from their exploring hands. Also she liked to keep it convenient, to have it close by when she needed an extra boost of energy to get through the mountain of household chores she faced each evening.

Susan's office job in the local school provided much-needed extra finance and meant that she was home at the same time as the children, but at this point in time she felt she couldn't catch up with herself in trying to cope with her many duties. A little drink in the evenings not only helped her to relax; she felt she actually needed it to keep her going.

An hour and a half later, awakened by Ed's insistent shake on her shoulder, Susan wasn't surprised that she was asleep at the kitchen table. After all 'it had been a long hard day, hadn't it?' she reasoned. She felt so tired now, all day long. In fact she found it hard to concentrate, to remember things.

The big question is at what point will Susan connect her behaviour and tiredness with her use of alcohol? At what point will she or Ed start to worry about her drinking? When will the question arise 'Is Susan an alcoholic?' After all so far, no one, not even her best friend, has seen her drunk. When Susan goes out socially, she drinks one or two glasses of wine, maybe a vodka or two; maybe she won't drink anything. And after all, Susan hasn't told anyone, not even herself, about how frightened she is that she can't seem to be able to do without those few drinks in the evening. Ed knows about the bottle in the cupboard but he doesn't know about the bottle in her boot at the back of her wardrobe. He doesn't know how desperately she needs to know that there is a drink there when she wants it. Neither does he know how often she replaces those bottles. Maybe he is starting to suspect it, but for now he isn't saying it. After all, the days are long and hard and everyone needs something to help them along.

• • •

Meanwhile on the other side of town Pat was also coming to the end of her long day. Pat was in bed. In fact she had been there since early afternoon. Pat lives on her own, her marriage having ended ten years ago, so there is no one there to shake her awake, to remind her to go to bed. Indeed there is no one there to remind her to get up in the morning. The one pressing engagement she has each day is with the local off-licence at the supermarket down the road. On her welfare days, after collecting her money, she stocks up on her supply, so she does not have to get up and go out the next day.

According to Pat she doesn't have a problem with alcohol. She likes it and why should she stop drinking? She isn't harming anyone. She has no friends anyway. Her one loyal companion is the booze in the bottles she keeps in the cupboard beside the bed.

Pat's flat is spotlessly clean. The windows sparkle. The curtains are frequently washed and rehung. Everything is spic and span. The smell of disinfectant and polish hang heavy in the air. The kitchen shines, all the utensils standing to attention on the white work surface. In the small living room the cushions sit welcomingly plumped up on the sofa. The place spells out comfort and respectability.

However, the neighbours and the local shopkeepers worry and talk anxiously about Pat and her stumbling, uncoordinated jaunts to the supermarket. 'Someone should do something,' they whisper. Smilingly unaware Pat returns home and quickly enters her bedroom where she gulps down a comfortingly warm swig from her bottle of Martini. She puts the bottle in the cupboard for the moment and is reassured by its presence. This room is different from the other rooms in her home. Along the wall is ranged a collection of empty brown, green and white bottles, while along the bordering wall is a long line of shiny empty cans. This is the room in which she lives. This is the room in which she drinks.

For Pat, there will be little difficulty in maintaining her alcoholism until she reaches the last hopelessly unmanageable stages when she will not be able to take care of herself. But at the moment her drinking does not seem a problem to her. She doesn't allow herself to even ask the question 'Am I an alcoholic'? That her life is dominated by a life-threatening and limiting illness has not been acknowledged by anyone, least of all herself.

• • •

Linda has had an interesting evening. She is going home, in a taxi, after a long session in one of the city's hot-spots. She hadn't intended to go out this evening but a couple of work colleagues had suggested a wind-down drink in a popular pub. She agreed to go for one drink, maybe two. Somehow the time passed and she had missed not only dinner, but also the early night she had promised herself.

Come to think of it, she had been promising herself that early night for quite a while now. 'Life's too short to miss,' she told herself as she ordered yet another drink from the barman and continued her conversation with the good-looking guy at the next table.

Linda has a well paid, demanding, responsible job in the money market. To be a heavy drinker is practically par for the course within her circle of friends. They work hard and they play hard and of course they drink hard too. Her friends do not even comment on the amount of alcohol she can consume at parties or social occasions. She is in demand as a drinking companion. She loves the crack and will always complete the course on any given evening. Linda will always agree to a suggestion to go on to a disco or night-club to have another drink. Successful and talented at her job, she is going places in her career. One must be seen in the right places, one must meet the right people, she reasons with herself.

However, recently Linda is feeling under pressure. She seems to be spending a lot of time watching the clock at work. Often she feels tired before she even starts and her head isn't as clear as it should be. Tonight as she is driven home, she avoids thinking of the hangover she will have tomorrow and the fact that she had promised herself that she would be well-rested for the important meeting in the morning. Maybe she'll take a couple of days' sick-leave; after all doesn't everyone? When she has had a rest, she'll make a new start. No more drinking during the week, only at weekends. Tonight was great fun, she tells herself. After all everyone else was drinking too!

Linda is secretly worried about her drinking. She feels it is slightly out of control. There have been too many broken promises to herself, too many embarrassing situations for her to ignore. However, no one else seems to notice. Her boss doesn't seem as happy with Linda's work as she used to be and Linda worries if maybe she isn't as capable or talented as had been thought. As yet her boss hasn't connected drinking with the variation in the quality of her work and Linda is trying not to make that connection herself. How could she be an alcoholic? She has a successful career and anyway she doesn't drink every day. Also she doesn't drink on her own. She only keeps the small bottle at the back of her drawer at work for emergencies, for those days when a hair of the dog makes it possible for her to concentrate on yet another interminable meeting.

One common illness

These three women have the same illness, hidden though that illness may be at the moment. They hide their worries and concerns about their drinking behind questions and justifications such as 'I don't drink enough to be an alcoholic'; 'I don't drink often enough to be an alcoholic'; 'I haven't been drinking long enough to be an alcoholic'; 'If I was an alcoholic, I couldn't hold down a job'.

Most people think they know the answer to the question 'What is an alcoholic'? Most people have their own descriptions and definitions of alcoholism. The confusion surrounding the nature of alcoholism leads to the possibility of avoiding and/or denying the existence of alcoholism in oneself or in the life of a loved one.

The World Health Organisation has defined an alcoholic in this way:

> Alcoholics are those excessive drinkers whose dependence on alcohol has attained such a degree that they show a noticeable mental disturbance or an interference with their mental and bodily health, their interpersonal relations and their smooth social and economic functioning; or who show the prodromal [warning] signs of such developments. They therefore require treatment.

In simple terms someone who is an alcoholic is someone who has a personal relationship with alcohol, a personal relationship which is sick. This is true in all and every case where there is alcoholism. The individual has a relationship with alcohol which has become sick, unhealthy, harmful to themselves, their families and to

13

other people closely associated with them.

Any of our relationships can become unhealthy. We can become sick in our relation to other people, in our love affairs. We can have sick relationships with power, sex, food, gambling, other drugs. Anything that is desirable to us can become the focus of our attention. It can start to preoccupy us, obsess us and we can develop a sick dependency relationship with it. We can become addicted to it.

The nature of the addiction

Addiction is not something mysterious, something totally removed from ordinary experience. It is a malignant outgrowth, an extreme, unhealthy manifestation of normal human inclinations. Addiction is not a chemical reaction. It is an experience which grows out of a person's response to something that has special meaning for her, to something that she finds so safe and reassuring that she cannot be without it.

An alcoholic is addicted to alcohol. Addiction is a dependency relationship which has become extreme and unhealthy, resulting in suffering, distress, harm and eventually death. Alcoholism is a specific addiction, a specific dependency relationship. It is a specific chemical dependency. Alcoholism is essentially 'a sick or pathological relationship of a person to a specific mood-altering chemical substance, alcohol, in expectation of a rewarding experience.' (Mc Auliffe and Mc Auliffe)

An alcoholic is a person who has a chemical dependency. She has developed a relationship with alcohol which has become extremely important to her. On one end of the relationship is an individual human person, on the other end is a powerful drug that can change significantly the way she feels, perceives and acts.

Alcohol abuse and dependency

Alcohol is desirable. It has a natural appeal because it offers the promise of a quick and welcome change of mood, mind and behaviour. Because every normal human being likes to feel better and to perceive and act differently at times, every normal person is a candidate for a relationship with alcohol. The misuse of alcohol occurs when there is a potential for harm in our use of it. The abuse of alcohol occurs when it brings actual harm or injury. Sometimes the harm may be relatively slight. Harm does not mean disaster and, unfortunately, the abuse of alcohol and other drugs is often only recognised when the results are approaching disaster.

Beyond alcohol abuse, indeed mostly right along side it, is alcohol dependency. The line between abuse and dependency, if it exists at all, is very fine indeed.

Consider the act of getting drunk, of losing control of one's judgement, concentration, body reactions and muscle control and co-ordination; even to the point sometimes of losing consciousness. Unquestionably this is alcohol abuse. Anybody can get drunk on rare occasions in spite of safeguards. Most people do not repeat unreasonable, harmful experiences. Repeated alcohol abuse to the state of intoxication is a clear sign of alcohol dependency. Alcohol abuse occurs when a person is acting by compulsion, not by reason or choice. The alcoholic person has developed an unhealthy need to drink alcohol in an irrational, unregulated and harmful way. She has developed an unhealthy or sick personal relationship with alcohol, a powerful mood-altering chemical.

Problem drinker/alcoholic?

When we try to distinguish between problem drinkers, heavy drinkers and alcoholics we run into problems. The distinction between one drinker and another is usually based on the particular circumstance of each individual person. The physical and social situation varies with each person as does the amount they drink, how often they drink, where they drink and who they drink with. However, the heavy use of alcohol and the problem use of alcohol is abuse; repeated abuse is a product of and a symptom of alcohol dependency, that is, of alcoholism. It doesn't matter how many people you are with, if you are drunk, you are drunk. There may be a hundred people around you also getting drunk or you may be alone. It makes no significant difference. You are abusing alcohol and if you do so repeatedly you are certainly alcohol dependent.

Social approval does not make alcohol abuse less harmful. A great number of people confuse social drinking with drinking in a situation where there is mutual encouragement of alcohol dependency. When you get drunk you are enjoying your relationship with drink first and foremost. Your enjoyment of other people comes second, if it matters at all. When someone is a 'social drinker' the alcohol use is incidental, its purpose being to enhance the pleasure of communication and social interchange. To get drunk is antisocial in that it always interferes in real and honest interpersonal relationships.

Am I an alcoholic?

The answer to 'Am I an alcoholic?' is not in how often you drink, how much you drink, what you drink or where you drink. Rather the answer is in the nature of your relationship with alcohol. Alcohol dependency is a deep personal commitment to alcohol for the sake of the rewards it brings; that is the high, the buzz, the euphoria or the change in mood you expect.

This means that if you are alcoholic, alcohol is the love of your life; you have developed and are developing a lasting, permanent relationship with alcohol. You are choosing for alcohol, finding time, money and energy to drink. What is motivating you is the change in mood alcohol promises you. Alcohol has promised you a guaranteed change in how you feel emotionally and physically and in how you think and act.

If you have experienced this as a rewarding experience, a welcome change, then you see alcohol in the role of, you believe, a constant and relatively cheap friend who will bring you comfort and relief with no hidden agenda, no strings attached. Such a relationship can begin innocently but if you become committed to it, it can soon be the most compulsive, demanding and overwhelming relationship in your life.

Chapter Two
Developing a relationship with alcohol

The prime motivation

Alcohol is a powerful mood-changer, and in time the need for alcohol is the prime motivator, the primary need in an individual's life if that person has a sick or unhealthy relationship with alcohol.

Initially, the nature of a person's relationship with alcohol may not be obvious and it may only emerge clearly as the illness progresses. In Susan, Pat and Linda's life, the true nature of their relationship with alcohol is emerging at different rates with varying degrees. However, for each one of them their focus, their main need, has become alcohol and what alcohol can do for them. How much they drink, how often they drink and what they drink are simply the symptoms of this primary relationship.

As the relationship develops it interferes with, precludes and overshadows more and more, the other relationships in their lives. It is usually at the late stages of the illness that alcoholism is recognised. However, the nature of the relationship with alcohol is present from the beginning. It is the commitment that marks the beginning of the alcoholism. Since this is in the person and not in the bottle, merely taking drink away or hiding it, even avoiding it, does not remove the alcoholism.

Often an individual is concerned about and focused on the 'why' of alcoholism. An alcoholic will often assume that there is another problem which is the cause of her drinking. 'If I had a family I wouldn't drink,' Pat says to herself. 'If I wasn't so tired and hadn't so much to do, I'd stop drinking,' Susan consoles herself. 'Anyway, Ed is never here and what else can I do?' Meanwhile Linda justifies her drinking by arguing 'I have to be able to relax after such a demanding job, and really I'm shy and I couldn't socialise without a drink.'

The other problems in an alcoholic's life are real and need to be dealt with. However, the prime motivation for drinking is always the expected mood change and this is true at all stages of alcoholism.

Alcoholism, a disease

Alcoholism has been recognised since the mid-fifties as a disease by major world health organisations. It is now generally acknowledged that the physical aspects of alcohol dependency are but part of a larger picture and are in fact later-stage developments in a process that has been going on in a person for some time, perhaps years, without obvious physical signs.

Complications such as brain and liver damage, acute withdrawal reactions and pancreatitis, are more usually late-stage physical aspects. Similarly character changes like paranoia and dysfunctional personal behaviour are late-stage psychological complications. Family and job problems, crime, driving while drunk are also late-stage social consequences of alcoholism. These are symptoms of an illness and more importantly are symptoms that are often only seen at the chronic or later-stage levels of alcoholism.

Again if you want an answer to the question 'Am I an alcoholic?' the focus must not be on the symptoms but on the underlying dependency, that is the nature of the relationship with alcohol. The symptoms may be very mild but the dependency may be already very well established. A person may ask 'Can I be an alcoholic?':

- If I don't get roaring drunk?
- If no one says anything to me?

- If I have never had an accident?
- If my liver isn't damaged?
- If I still have a job?
- If I don't drink on my own?
- If my family don't object?
- If my drinking companions drink as much as me?
- If I can stop drinking for a time?

The answer is most definitely yes, because the dependence may already have taken hold.

Alcohol dependency and women

Alcoholism, or alcohol dependency as it is now known, is a complex and baffling illness. It is widely considered to be multi-dimensional and cultural factors are thought to combine in producing an individual who is vulnerable to alcohol dependency. Current thinking, the culmination of years of research attempting to make sense of these factors, recognises that the discovery of a single explanatory cause is highly improbable. There is no simple explanation for the fact that for some people their relationship with alcohol becomes more than casual and results in the loss of the key elements of choice and balance.

For these individuals a relational decision to keep alcohol use within set limits eg, only after 6 pm or only at weekends, has no effect when the compulsion or desire to drink takes over. A Chinese proverb says, 'First the woman takes a drink; then the drink takes a drink; finally, the drink takes the woman.' Alcoholics are people who have lost control and their need for drink becomes a physical demand. Even when deep down they know that alcohol is causing problems they still desperately desire the illusory freedom, contentment and independence expected from it.

The promise of avoiding pain, tension, worry, hurt and other uncomfortable feelings and the promise of experiencing warmth, pleasure, release or happiness, however fleeting, is too inviting for these women and they try to ignore the guilt, shame and desperation that results.

Increasingly their relationship with alcohol brings conflict due to the choices made in favour of alcohol at the price of corroding other personal values and relationships.

In an attempt to protect the love affair with alcohol, a woman will bring all her emotional, intellectual and spiritual forces to bear on the situation. Alcohol becomes more and more the centre of the alcoholic's life, more and more the centre of her thoughts, wishes and desires. She will justify and defend her placing of drink at the core of her personal values, standards and needs and she will attempt to ward off any threat to her love affair with alcohol, in any way she can.

Personality changes

So, Susan, Pat and Linda justify to themselves their desire to drink, they hide the extent of their drinking from those around them and they deny to themselves and others their difficulties and problems with alcohol. A change in their personality, in their personal beliefs, values and choices, is already developing. The scene is set for painful negative emotions to increase. Behaving in ways they previously would not have behaved, like, Pat's staying in bed all day; Susan not being willing to relate to Ed at an emotional or sexual level; Linda's not turning up at work, gives rise to feelings of shame, guilt, remorse, self-hatred and lowered self-esteem. In this situation alcohol is even more attractive and a vicious circle begins. They feel bad and they want to drink. They drink and they feel worse. They want to drink again.

The false promise of the bottle

The very issues which for these women may have made alcohol attractive – their sense of weakness, incompetence, fear of failure, fear of loneliness are compounded and aggravated by their drinking. These women had needs and alcohol offered them an answer. Alcohol is a depressant drug. It inhibits reflexes and sensitivity to outside stimulation. It is a blanket of comfort from the world. The soothing feeling that all is well is a powerful experience and is particularly attractive to women who believe themselves to be inadequate and are looking for something to ease the pain of this belief.

No one is safe from the line of this false promise. No one is ever too young, too old, too successful or too busy to become alcoholic. Exposing yourself to the risk of dependency occurs insofar as you abuse alcohol on a regular or recurrent basis. As more women drink, more women risk developing alcohol problems. It is certainly true that more women are now drinking openly. It is generally acknowledged that the real numbers of alcoholic women are unknown. Alcoholism is still a widespread but misunderstood and hidden illness. Alcoholics tend to minimise and hide the extent of their drinking. There is a high percentage of secret drinkers among women in particular. Women who drink at home, alone, are a suffering silent segment of our population.

Habits of dependency are learned by growing up in a culture which teaches personal inadequacies, a reliance on external factors to effect change and a sense of hopelessness or despair. A potential alcoholic starts with a low opinion of herself. She has not learned to accomplish things she can regard as worthwhile, or to even enjoy life. An alcoholic becomes increasingly dependent on alcohol as her only source of gratification. Forgetfulness is the one aim she is capable of pursuing wholeheartedly. This has significance for women, who fit the above scenario with particular ease due to social and cultural mores and pressures in western societies.

It has been widely documented in mental health literature that groups in society who are devalued or lack control over their lives are particularly prone to depression and other emotional problems. For women, more than men, studies have shown that alcoholism often follows the onset of depression or emotional problems. Alcohol abuse may represent one of the many mechanisms by which women attempt to cope with their experienced or perceived helplessness or lack of control in their personal lives. Unfortunately, this traps them into a situation of less, rather than more, personal freedom and power, robbing them of the remnants of self-esteem, and reducing their actual capacity to effect change.

Seeking help

Availability of alcohol for women and the numbers of women now drinking may have changed but underlying attitudes towards women and alcohol have not altered as quickly. Alcoholism is still considered a moral issue by many. Women are still judged more harshly than men. If an alcoholic man is considered weak-willed, an alcoholic woman is branded immoral, promiscuous, selfish, irresponsible, unfeminine, even unnatural. As a result, women avoid seeking help in order to avoid disapproval or censure. They hide their drinking because of their sense of shame. They tend to drink in secret and become stuck in rigid denial of their illness. The consequences to themselves and others of attempting to avoid their feelings of failure, shame and fear are often great indeed.

However, a woman with alcohol problems may seek help for related difficulties such as sleeplessness, financial difficulties, marital instability, feelings of unhappiness and depression, headaches, problems with children, an inability to concentrate. She will visit marriage counsellors, therapists, clergymen and doctors, most of whom know little about alcoholism and are unlikely to identify her problem with alcohol. Indeed, doctors often mis-diagnose a woman's alcoholism as nerves or depression and may prescribe a psychoactive drug such as valium or librium. She will emerge from her doctor's office not only with her alcoholism still unidentified but also with a second potentially addictive drug in her hand. She is on the road to extending her dependency on mood-altering chemicals to include not only alcohol but other drugs.

Dangers of cross-addiction

The reality is that women are habitual, frequent users of prescribed drugs to a greater degree than men. They are at risk of combining alcohol with tranquillisers. Amphetamines, anti-depressants and other prescribed drugs to ease the pain of boredom, tension, fatigue, too much pressure and loneliness are often used by alcoholics. When alcohol interacts with another drug in the body it may result in a reduction of the effects of either or both drugs. On the other hand it may produce an added effect in which the total effect of the drugs is greater. This is highly dangerous and is most clearly exemplified by the combination of alcohol and barbiturates where from which difficulty in breathing may result.

Chronic alcohol use can produce tolerance to alcohol and also a diminished responsiveness to other drugs. Cross-tolerance, as this is called, does not require previous exposure to the second drug. Thus alcoholics are more difficult to anaesthetise with ether than non-alcoholics.

Mixing of drugs is dangerous. A woman with alcohol dependency is already dependent on a mood-altering chemical and is therefore almost programmed to extend her expectation of a mood change to any other drug.

There are clearly defined stages in the progress of a woman to acute alcoholism. The next chapter will show these stages and explain how a woman can become an alcoholic over a short period of time, with disastrous results to her health, personal relationships and, ultimately, her life.

Chapter Three
Stages of progressive alcoholism

Imagine a destructive and fatal disease, a disease of unknown origin, which comes to public awareness; a disease so harmful to the nervous system that people all over the country, many thousands of them, go crazy for periods, lasting from a few hours to weeks or months. Imagine that this craziness or insanity recurs repeatedly for years and becomes increasingly long-lasting and eventually permanent.

Imagine that during such periods of insanity these people behaved in a destructive manner so as to harm themselves and their families physically, mentally, emotionally, and financially; that they place whole groups of individuals at risk; their work in industry, in business, in their professions and in their homes becomes crippled, sabotaged, totally neglected.

Finally, imagine that their judgement and awareness becomes so distorted and clouded that they cannot or will not believe that they have a disease, that they deny or ignore the evidence of what is happening around them, and that in fact their judgement becomes so perverted that they want this disease to continue.

Surely if such a disease were to appear it would be reacted to with horror and shock. It would be declared a disaster, an international catastrophe; there would be a demand for research to explore the cause of the disease and a treatment for it; huge efforts would be made to provide rehabilitation for the sufferers and their families. Yes? Well, no actually. This is not a science fiction fantasy, or a story of a virus spread by aliens to cripple, undermine and limit the potential of the human race. This disease is already here in our midst, as many tragically know and as many more tragically are trying to avoid knowing. This disease is alcoholism.

Who are alcoholics and where do they come from? They are from all backgrounds, environments, races, religions and lifestyles. They are of every age; from the fifteen-year-old schoolgirl who gets drunk at every opportunity, telling herself she is having a great time, that she is really independent, grown-up and cool; to the twenty-five-year-old career woman who wakes up in the morning beside a man she has never seen before; to the thirty-five-year-old housewife with five children, who takes a 'little drink' in the afternoon to relax before the children come home from school and ends up asleep on the sofa before tea-time; to the forty-five-year-old socialite who gives marvellous dinner parties and tries to forget the embarrassing ending of such evenings; to the fifty-five-year-old woman who has reared her children and relieves the tedium and boredom of her life by drinking bottles of sherry every day; to the sixty-five-year-old woman who lives alone and goes to the pub to drink bottles of stout in the snug, telling herself she needs company, but ends up staggering home alone to her messy, cold flat.

The alcoholic is everywhere. She is the woman bringing her children to school, the teacher who teaches your children, the woman who cuts your hair, the woman in the local shop, your doctor, your solicitor, your neighbour, your wife, mother, lover, sister, friend or daughter. She might even be you.

Symptoms of alcoholism

Very few women alcoholics fit the common, stereotyped image of the drunk; you know the type seen in films, the slightly seedy run-down woman who slurps whiskey on a bar stool while ogling the men; or the haggard wretch who walks the streets with her brown paper bag, sleeping at nights in parks and derelict buildings. These women do exist but they account for only about 3 per cent of alcoholics. They are the exception rather than the rule.

So many people say 'She/I can't be an alcoholic; because an alcoholic

- drinks all day
- is drunk all the time
- will drink anything, even meths
- has to drink the next day
- doesn't have hangovers.

The variations are endless. However, these are symptoms of the final and most visible stages of the disease. Before reaching this stage most women alcoholics either seek treatment or die. How many obituaries report heart failure, car accident, respiratory failure or suicide when the real cause of death is alcoholism? Because it is such a cunning, hidden disease, so often the consequences are not recognised as being the results of a disease.

That alcoholism is a disease seems undeniable. Alcoholism, or alcohol dependency as it is now known, is not just a symptom of another problem or disease but the root cause of the behavioural, emotional and spiritual problems experienced; it has identifiable symptoms and consequences. Millions of pounds have been spent, to no avail, on research attempting to show that alcoholism is a symptom. No research has ever causally related it to any given event, personality trait or character type. No one knows for sure why some people develop this illness; it cannot yet be predicted who will become alcoholic. Because only alcoholics whose disease has progressed to the later stages are available for study and observation, very frequently the effects of the disease are mistaken for the causes.

Often family members describe the alcoholic as 'a very irresponsible person', 'someone with no heart', 'lacking in self esteem', 'a born liar', 'selfish to the core', 'disorganised', 'cunning and dishonest', 'distant and cold', 'very shy and fearful', 'a Jekyll and Hyde', 'a street angel and house devil', 'living in cloud cuckoo land', 'totally undependable'.

They see these descriptions and similar ones as being personality traits and they fail to realise that the woman's addiction is already firmly in place and that these characteristics and patterns of behaviour are actually *symptoms* of the illness. This is because the addiction progressively dominates the individual's choices and dictates her behaviour. Alcoholics thus come to appear more and more similar to other alcoholics. This makes the progression of the illness very predictable. Because of the conflicts between alcoholics' values and their actual behaviour, alcoholics become irresponsible, devious, evasive, defensive, irrational and often obnoxious. This is not *why* they are alcoholic. This is *because* they are alcoholic.

Possible causes of alcoholism

While research shows no clear psychological or sociological determinants of alcoholism, it does indicate some genetic or inherited factors. The children of alcoholic parents are at least four times more likely to develop the disease. It has been shown that identical twins of alcoholic parents, separated and adopted at birth to non-alcoholic homes, are more likely to become alcoholic. However, the identical twins of non-alcoholic parents, separated and adopted at birth to alcoholic homes, are less likely to develop alcoholism. This seems to indicate that genetic factors are an important element.

A child growing up with alcoholic parents is more likely to develop alcoholism than a child growing up in a non-alcoholic home. The effects of emotional neglect, even abuse, the confusion between what is happening and what the child is told, the lack of communication about feelings, the mood swings, the irrational thinking, the inconsistent and unpredictable behaviour of a parent leads to unmet needs in the child of an alcoholic. These unmet emotional needs seem to place them at risk of developing alcoholism later in life.

Because of the confusion about what alcoholism is, who

can become alcoholic and why people become alcoholic, families regularly do not recognise the illness in its early stages. When you place the lack of knowledge and understanding side by side with the still existing prejudice against women who drink, and the denial by the alcoholic herself, it is not surprising that so often this disease goes undiagnosed and its progression remains unhindered.

Alcoholism often develops slowly (though this is not always the case). The love relationship with the bottle gradually and surely intensifies and becomes increasingly important. Alcohol dependency does not spring into existence overnight, fully developed. Unlike a mushroom which appears magically in the morning, an addiction has to be nurtured and cultivated for a period of time. The length of time varies from one woman to another. An addiction has deep roots and a strong hold on a woman by the time those around her become aware of the changes in her or begin to acknowledge the seriousness and permanency of these changes.

The progressive stages

There are four stages in the development of alcoholism. The sufferer moves from the pre-alcoholic phase to the pre-prodromal or warning stage, to the phase of loss of control, and finally to the chronic phase of total alcohol dependency.

Often women think that alcoholism is beginning when they first become aware of problems associated with drinking. Family members, friends and other concerned persons believe the illness is starting only when they see a change in the woman's drinking pattern, in her way of living, or in her personal or social behaviour. They will describe the alcoholism as beginning at the stage when they notice she is drinking more, drinking more often, or drinking alone. They see the alcoholism as beginning when the woman starts to get drunk more easily, due to lowered tolerance to alcohol, when she can only drink a few vodkas and sounds slurred, or becomes aggressive, rather than being able to drink all night as she used to.

Some people talk about the alcoholism beginning from the time the woman withdraws from other people or loses interest in her appearance, in her hobbies, or in looking after her home. They start to wonder about alcoholism when she starts to look thinner, when she becomes careless about her dress, when her skin coarsens, her pores enlarge, her complexion becomes ruddy or yellowy or her face becomes bloated and tired looking. They focus on the visible signs and changes and believe these to be the illness rather than understanding that these changes are the signs of a disease that has been present for some time.

Such changes and problems do not happen overnight. In their search for an explanation or justification for these unavoidable indications of something being very wrong, women and their families often relate the drinking to events occurring at the time when the drinking becomes more obviously problematic. They often then come to believe that alcoholism is due to marital problems, bereavements, financial pressures, illness or 'nerves' problems. Women alcoholics typically describe a recent loss or family crisis as precipitating alcoholic drinking. This may partly be due to the woman's need to alleviate her shame at admitting her dependency, especially because of the greater stigma attached to a woman being an alcoholic.

The crises women cite most often as contributing to their drinking are divorce/separation, death of a family member, a child leaving home, menstrual difficulties, menopause and depression after pregnancy and childbirth. It is interesting that these crises mostly relate to functions seen as defining the traditional female role. Since women still identify themselves primarily through these functions, any occurrences which intensify feelings of inadequacy in these areas would of course be experienced as very threatening. A crises does seem to speed up the progression of alcoholism into another stage of the illness; a woman's drinking may be accelerated at this point.

However, the alcohol dependency, that is, her unhealthy relationship with alcohol in the expectation of a rewarding experience, is already present and germinating. What changes in a time of crisis is that the reward alters; the mood change sought has moved from pleasure to relief from pain, or from relief to just coping or surviving.

This desire for the effect which alcohol can bring her is the main motivation that leads a woman into alcoholism, and also keeps her there. The progression of the disease can be seen in the change in the type of effect wanted or expected from the alcohol. This hope and anticipation of a change in mood and feeling is an extremely powerful force. It is so powerful that a high can often be experienced even from a substitution. For example, take the situation of Sandra who had set up a pattern of hope and anticipation long before she developed the symptoms of alcoholism. Picture her as a fifteen-year-old girl, drinking with her friends every Saturday. She looks forward all week to the night out. What she will wear, how she will dress, her hair, these are major worries. Who will be there, what band will be playing, are always interesting topics. The night arrives, seats in the bar are taken, the drinks ordered. Sandra is having her favourite tipple, vodka and orange juice. The evening moves on and the order is renewed from the barman, 'Same again, Tom!' After a couple of drinks Sandra is quite tipsy, feeling giddy and talkative. What Sandra hasn't realised is that Tom the barman misheard the order. She has only had two orange juices but her expectation of a high is so great that she experiences it anyway.

Often astonishment and amazement is expressed at how alcoholics can continue the destructive pattern of drinking despite the misery they experience, the physical discomfort, the shame and guilt, the humiliations, the disapproval and disgust of others and the disasters they experience due to their behaviour. 'Why can't she ever learn?' is a constant refrain; 'Surely this will stop her?' another. 'How can she go on drinking now?' baffled family members ask. As the disease progresses the alcoholic does not learn from mistakes, broken relationships, horrifying accidents, painful illnesses and deteriorating health. Instead she tries to relieve her anxiety and worry. She attempts to medicate her feelings by drinking; she seeks after relief rather than pleasure. The hope and anticipation of a change in her mood drives her on regardless of the cost. By the time alcohol is no longer providing the hoped-for high, the commitment to search for relief from tiredness, sleeplessness, anxiety, frustration, loneliness, grief, sadness, feelings of insecurity and inadequacy has already begun.

• • •

How did Susan, Pat, and Linda, whom we met in Chapter One, fall into their self-imposed traps? We will look at the progressive stages of their common illness now.

SUSAN

Susan started drinking in her late teens. She didn't touch alcohol for the first couple of years when out socialising and dancing with her friends. In fact she was quite uncomfortable around people who had been drinking. She knew how alcohol changed a person's personality and mood, and the way it often allowed them to speak and behave in ways which were not reliable. She did not trust alcohol nor did she trust people when they were drinking. She knew this about alcohol because her own father had been a heavy drinker; indeed he was an alcoholic though she was not aware of this and would have been surprised if anyone had described him as such. His behaviour and pattern of drinking were all she had ever known and had been the norm for her growing up. Susan had many feelings of anger, shame and hurt about the way he had treated her mother and the family.

As time progressed Susan's fear of alcohol lessened and as one by one her friends began to drink alcohol and to enjoy it, Susan became more curious and even a little embarrassed at not drinking. She was a shy person and was quite inhibited at the best of times in social gatherings. So, eventually one evening Susan took a sweet martini to fit in with the crowd. She was interested to find out if she too could become more sociable, more fun and more at ease by drinking. After all, hadn't she watched her friends appear to have great fun from drinking alcohol and even getting a little drunk. Susan became a little tipsy that evening and her friends ribbed her quite a bit, in a good humoured way, about having too much to drink. She felt she *belonged* in a new way and had another bond with her friends. Alcohol became part of the social round and soon a night out wasn't quite right without several drinks — vodka or rum. Susan left martini behind quite early on. 'It's too sweet and makes me feel sick,' she told herself as she moved on to more potent mixtures.

During those years of parties, pubs and discos Susan met Ed. He moved in the same circle and they soon started going out together. Life didn't change much for either of them despite their new relationship. Most of their social outings centred around alcohol. They met in the pub, went drinking before and after the cinema; before and during dances; before and after dinner dates. For Susan, alcohol was now a constant in her life. A constant she depended on to bring relaxation, freedom, fun and social ease to her life. She didn't notice Ed's relationship with alcohol because she was too focused on her own. She didn't object to going to the pub all the time because she felt more comfortable there. In fact, even their sexual relationship centred around alcohol. Having a few drinks first made Susan feel uninhibited and more relaxed. There was no harm in a few drinks to 'lubricate the proceedings', she told herself.

The pre-alcoholic phase

Susan experienced a great 'kick' from her initial experiences with alcohol. She got a certain 'something' from it. She liked the feeling and she continued to drink. She didn't in the beginning seek out opportunities to drink deliberately, but rather, she casually continued to drink alcohol. This remained a pleasurable activity. With the pleasure came subsequent passing memories and reflections on these occasions and eventually she developed a planned, premeditated desire to get high. With this subtle decision to continue to drink alcohol, to get drunk, in order to have this high, Susan moved into a commitment to relying on a chemical, alcohol, to change her mood. As she sought the pleasant mood-swings more and more, her experience of them left deeper and deeper impressions on her mind.

The warning signs

Alcohol had now become the centre of many pleasurable memories, thoughts and fantasies. In this lay the seeds of a preoccupation that could become an obsession. Repeated drinking occasions became regular. It was an easy step for Susan to move from drinking when happy, to drinking to become happy, to drinking on various occasions to allay her feelings of anxiety, fear, disappointment, tension, sorrow. Drinking is now her standard means of handling stress as well as a way of finding pleasure. Susan's drinking does not *look* any different to other people's. No one around Susan noticed that she was in the initial stages of alcohol dependency.

Similarly no one noticed much when Susan's tolerance rose and she appeared to be able to drink more without apparent ill-effect. When Susan began to 'sneak' a few drinks *before* dinner at friends' homes, or to have a couple of drinks *before* leaving her own house when she knew it would be a 'quiet' evening, or to gulp down the first drink or two at a party, no one seemed to notice.

Then, Susan began to have the odd blackout. The first couple of times this was a great joke between herself and Ed; she couldn't remember what she had said or where they had gone or who had said what. They made a joke of it, 'I said what!?' she would exclaim. But when the blackouts continued Susan kept quiet and pretended that she could remember parts of a particular evening that in fact were completely blank in her memory. No one seemed to notice, not even Ed. She had looked all right, well, maybe a bit tipsy or jarred, but she acted normally enough. Susan became an expert at asking the right questions, piecing bits of information together so that no one guessed.

Her guilt and fear and conflicting feelings about her drinking were also beginning to increase. Neither Susan, nor Ed (her husband by now), nor her friends realised that she had moved from the **pre-alcoholic phase** to the **prodromal phase** (meaning warning or signalling disease). Though she *was* drinking a lot it was not conspicuous. Freedom to drink casually or socially had steadily yielded to stronger and stronger feelings of urgency or compulsion to drink. Susan, or any other drinker, could remain at this phase of alcohol dependency for a shorter, perhaps six-month, period or a longer, perhaps five-year period, depending on circumstances.

Loss of control

Susan has had three children, one after another. Now, after an attempt to address her feelings of inadequacy, self-hatred, guilt, shame and remorse about the frequent bouts of drinking alone in the evening, she has taken up a part-time job. Susan does not realise it but she has entered the third crucial phase of alcohol dependency, **loss of control**. Now she reaches into the cupboard for her vodka, despite all the excuses and justifications she makes even to herself about the amount she will drink. She can no longer decide 'I'll have one, or two, or three drinks tonight.' No longer can she be sure what state she will finish up in. She has reached the stage of loss of control and all her promises and resolutions, even to herself, mean nothing. She has continually broken them. She has repeatedly ended up stupid drunk when she had told herself she was only having one or two or three drinks, despite her excuses to herself that she needs a drink 'to give me energy' or that she deserves it 'because it's been a hard day'.

Susan feels demoralised, discouraged and ashamed of her failure. She is alternatively remorseful, resentful and at times aggressive to her family. She has much conflict between her actual behaviour and how she thinks she should act. She copes with this by blocking from her memory the blackouts, the drinking to unconsciousness, the nasty, uncomfortable details of her life. She denies to herself as well as to others, the role that alcohol now plays in her life. She denies her love relationship with drink, her dependency on alcohol. She denies the problems alcohol is causing her. She stops drinking for periods in an attempt to convince herself that she can control it. But when she starts again, she still cannot control the amount she drinks. She attempts various strategies like: 'If I just drink after 9 pm it will be okay.' 'If I just drink sherry, it will be okay.' 'If I just drink at weekends, it will be okay.' 'If I just drink with Ed, it will be okay.'

Of course for Susan it is never okay. She becomes increasingly preoccupied and anxious. She loses interest in her ICA meetings, in her badminton club, in the children's sports. She increasingly avoids her neighbours and friends. When they call to the door she pretends she is not in and doesn't answer. She lets her garden deteriorate rather than work in it and perhaps have to talk to the neighbours. She likes people less and less and feels irritable, edgy and impatient with them. Her job is at risk because of the poor quality of her work and her sullen and unsociable manner. Money is increasingly a worry due to the amount she is spending daily on alcohol. Susan drinks rather than eats now, and so she is tired, depressed and lethargic. She tells herself it is the pressures of married life, of a family, of being a working mother. Anything rather than admit to herself that she is alcoholic.

Approaching the chronic stage

Susan now drinks vodka in a mug from the bottle stored behind the disinfectant, 'to protect the children', while doing her evening chores. She is moving steadily towards **chronic alcoholism**. It has taken her many years to reach this stage. Her neighbours and friends do not recognise her illness. Her husband attempts to protect her by being supportive rather than acknowledging the role of alcohol in her life, and she herself is busily denying her alcoholism. Nonetheless, Susan is alcohol dependent. She is frequently using alcohol to deal with her everyday stress. She is drinking more and more, gradually larger amounts. She is drinking alone and she is trying to hide the drinking from the children, from her friends, workmates, neighbours, family, even from Ed. She has lost time from work (though she tells herself it is because she is sick or too tired or entitled to the odd day off). She gets upset when her drinking is questioned, complained about or even referred to. She has been making promises to 'drink less', 'drink different types of alcohol', 'behave better', and asks Ed to be reasonable and understanding and to stop nagging her.

At times Susan denies she is drinking, even though she looks intoxicated or red-eyed or tired and Ed is convinced she has been. She has refused to face up to her responsibilities. She is not paying bills on time, not keeping contact with the school and she has lost interest in her own non-drinking activities. She has also lost interest in Ed's job. She is more concerned about her own problems. Increasingly she is irritable, moody, defensive, argumentative, jealous and easily angered, especially when drinking. Often the children know by her mood whether or not she is drinking. Arguments are beginning to develop, not only about her drinking. She is avoiding friends and social activities (though they don't realise that).

Susan has physical symptoms that are related to her alcohol abuse. She has become inefficient, fatigued. She has less energy and more sleepless nights. She has lost weight and frequently has accidents around the house. Her family and friends are worried about her. She feels increasingly bad about herself and is guilty, and depressed.

The picture becomes clearer when the pieces of the jigsaw are put together, but though all the pieces are there, no one in Susan's life has yet realised that she desperately needs help. She has a progressive, incurable disease and unless someone directs her to seek help, she will deteriorate further, with much distress and sorrow for those who care about her. She is now out of control and unable to stop drinking without help.

Even *one* of the above signs is enough to indicate a possible drinking problem and to signal the need for prompt help. Her family and friends, like many other people, do not realise this. Meanwhile Susan continues her solitary drinking unhindered, and even her bin-men don't realise that the garbage contains many vodka bottles wrapped in newspaper to stop them rattling.

PAT

Pat also had a part-time job. Like Susan she had managed to keep her alcoholism secret from those around her. With her spotless, comfortable little flat, her job and her bridge friends once weekly, people assumed that Pat was content and managing. It was tragic of course about her husband. (They were separated. He had left her suddenly.) Kindly neighbours made it their business to always greet Pat, realising that she must be lonely though she showed no obvious signs of distress. Also like Susan, Pat's drinking had been slowly progressing over the years until inevitably her life had become drink-centred.

Living to drink

Pat had reached the point where she too was living to drink. Her day revolved around her private and solitary consumption of several alcoholic drinks every evening. She was neglecting other interests and cutting herself off from people who were too close for comfort. Her contact with family and friends gradually diminished. Pat started to experience a decrease in her tolerance for alcohol. It took less alcohol to make her drunk and she began to experience tremors in her hands and edginess in her stomach when she hadn't had a drink for a while. She started to take a drink in the morning so that she could face the day and the people in her day. The thoughts of living in her flat without a drink soon became intolerable and before long not only was Pat taking a drink to cure her early morning shakes, she would have several more by lunch-time.

In the chronic phase

Up to then Pat had prided herself on the fact that she only drank *after* lunch. Her last remnant of self respect was shredded and she became extremely demoralised. 'What's the point?' she asked herself. 'Who cares anyway?' she thought, as she pulled away from contact with other people. She decided to give up her afternoon job in the local council offices. Pat has now moved into the final **chronic phase** of alcohol dependency. All alibis about her relationship with alcohol have been exhausted and her real dependency on it is now obvious. She has decided to devote her life to the vain pursuit of some indefinable relief that she hopes alcohol will give her. Intoxication for her is now an almost daily, day-long phenomenon, interrupted only by lack of money. She now drinks the cheapest of brands, indeed is prepared to sample any substitute available.

Pat is now living alone, only going out for necessities. She spends most of her time in her bedroom, usually in bed. Her tolerance for alcohol has dropped sharply which means she gets quite stupefied after only a small amount of alcohol. She has tremors and shakes when not drinking. Indeed even simple tasks are now difficult for her when she is sober. She is full of fear and anxiety. She is still denying her alcoholism, even though she regards alcohol as her best friend, a guaranteed friend, a friend whose reassurance, comfort and company is dependable, constant and relatively cheap.

Drinking to live

For Pat this life is safe, no strings attached, a much easier one than the challenge of human relationships. She doesn't want to realise that her physical health, social life, spiritual life and mental abilities have all been curtailed and deeply affected by her relationship with alcohol. She doesn't want to know about her alcoholism because the one thing that Pat believes makes life bearable is her drink. She is now drinking to live, as she sees it. She is a chronic alcoholic.

● ● ●

Susan's and Pat's stories exemplify the progression of alcohol dependency. Every individual's disease follows approximately this pattern. Circumstances, life situation, personality and age may differ, but the alcoholic's relationship with alcohol is qualitatively the same. Any of the signs or symptoms outlined above, if observed in your life or in a friend's or relative's life, are warnings and indications that alcoholism may be a cause for concern.

If this is the case the problem will not go away. Alcoholism is a progressive illness from which there is no cure but from which thousands of people recover every year. The stages and phases of this illness were first charted in 1952 by E. M. Jellinek. His work described the pattern of symptoms and the increasing dysfunction in the lives of alcoholics. Despite the differences between the individuals he observed (all members of Alcoholics

Anonymous) the similarities were remarkable just like those in Pat's or Susan's case.

The beginnings of change

The first stop in arresting the progress of alcoholism is to become aware of its presence in a person's life and to admit the serious and fundamental nature of the illness. Ignoring alcoholism, pretending it isn't there, turning a blind eye to problems incurred, smoothing out the uncomfortable consequences for the alcoholic, simply provides a safe haven for the disease to gain a further hold. One of the most important advantages of knowing the stages of the disease is that it helps us recognise that it is alcoholism we are dealing with. However it is essential for all involved to know that it is not necessary for someone to go through all the stages of the disease before treatment is possible.

There is no need for any woman to lose as much as Susan or Pat have before help is offered to them. The sooner we have the courage to honestly chart the different aspects of our own drinking or that of a loved one's drinking and realistically acknowledge any changes or deterioration such as those illustrated by Susan's and Pat's experiences, the sooner recovery can begin. Remember, not every alcoholic looks obviously drunk at any stage. There are nearly as many drinking patterns as there are alcoholics. But there are warning signs as Susan's and Pat's stories show.

The tragedy of denial

Women can drink themselves into alcoholism without really perceiving that they have become addicted. For some women the deterioration in their quality of life will be noticed by family and friends who will connect these changes with their relationship with alcohol. This can be difficult and upsetting for concerned family and friends who sometimes feel they are betraying their mother, sister, wife, lover or friend. It can be difficult and shameful for a husband to admit that his wife is having an affair, a committed love relationship, with the bottle of alcohol she tries to hide in their home. It can be painful and humiliating for a child to admit that her mother loves her vodka more than she loves her. It can be shocking and saddening for a woman to admit that her friend cares more for a drink than she does about their friendship.

The shame, despair and deep guilt that an alcoholic woman feels about her continuing failures to control her drinking, to manage her affairs, to maintain any standards or values in her work and home, to her colleagues, friends, children or husband lead to strong denial of both the alcoholism and its consequences for all around her. This denial is probably the most characteristic and most baffling symptom of the disease.

Discovering the truth

Some women's alcoholism comes to light when they have a physical illness or injury, the nature or circumstance of which may prompt the doctor to question her about drinking. She may have had an accident and appear intoxicated at a hospital. She may have a gastric ulcer or other conditions which alcohol can cause. Or it may be discovered in routine checks that she has an enlarged liver or abnormal levels of alcohol in her blood. However, the frequency with which alcohol is consumed and the quantity consumed is easily disguised or lied about. Rarely does the illness for which the woman is hospitalised show the true nature of her dependency. Unless withdrawal symptoms are recognised, it can easily be missed. Another possible way by which alcoholism is revealed is through financial entanglements such as borrowing money and developing debts to financial institutions. Similarly, legal complications such as drinking and driving prosecutions can show up the problem. A final area where alcoholism may be discovered is the work place.

LINDA

The warning signs

Linda has started to demonstrate alcohol-related problems in her work, though there are no obvious indications in other areas of her life. While her supervisor's evaluation of her work is still favourable, it is really an inflated estimation of her actual job performance, based on her potential abilities and previous reputation. Linda, a financial consultant in her mid-twenties, loves her job and is good at it. She is in the early stages of alcohol dependency and has justified her drinking by explaining it away in a social context. She ignores the personal and private investment she has in the pleasurable mood-changes alcohol gives her. She hides the extent of her drinking by mixing with a group of individuals who drink heavily in the socially acceptable environment of a club or hotel.

At risk in the workplace

Linda is worried about her work. She knows her drive, energy and interest are waning. She is sometimes late back after lunch and on occasion she has left work early. Under the guise of sickness she has started to lose time due to drinking. Her fellow workers have not yet officially complained but there is bad feeling between her and her closest co-worker. This bad feeling is due to her mood swings and sensitivity to any criticism, real or imagined. Her judgement has been affected and she has been known to lie about circumstances surrounding questionable decisions. Her efficiency has decreased and she has already missed a deadline for an important project. This reflects badly through association on her co-worker and has led to difficulties in team-work.

There are many ways in which alcoholism can affect attendance, job performance, attitude and manner at work.

As the disease progresses more time is lost due to vague ailments, implausible reasons are offered and some time off is usually taken, even without explanation. Linda's ability to perform deteriorates as her physical health, concentration, memory and other mental abilities become more impaired. Eventually this results in either criticism from management and disciplinary action or else Linda will just fail to advance in her job. Others will receive the promotions she desires.

For some alcoholics work is the one area they will protect and defend against alcohol-induced problems. This is because a successful career can bolster a damaged self-image which is being further undermined by the powerlessness experienced due to drinking-associated problems. Also, work is the source of the money supply which provides the alcohol.

For Linda, however, her job is probably her best opportunity for early intervention. There is great leverage there to halt her alcoholism because of her ambition and one-time enthusiasm for her career. If she is lucky the connection between her job deterioration and her drinking will be made by her boss or her personnel officer and the observations will be acted on.

• • •

Let us hope that for Susan, Pat and Linda some concerned person, or they themselves, will halt the progression of alcohol dependency in their lives before they reach the terminal stage where a woman gives up on herself and there is total disintegration of her sense of identity and worth. In the final stages a woman will either be so full of despair and not want to live, or be so physically and mentally damaged, she will not be able to make decisions necessary to maintain her life. In the first case she may either consciously decide to end her life or more usually she starts to drink to oblivion. In other words, she escapes into daily stupefication or unconsciousness.

In this last stage the alcoholic is abusing drink in a

manner that makes her existence a living death. It is very important to recognise the effect the chemical alcohol has on the body and the mind. Chapter Four explains the physical and mental deterioration which is very much an ignored part of progressive alcohol abuse.

Chapter Four
The physical effects

When a woman is alcohol dependent, or alcoholic, she is dependent on, or addicted to, a drug called ethyl alcohol or ethanol. Often people are shocked by the terms addict or addiction, but abuse of a range of addicting chemicals has been with us since history began. There has never been a culture where people have not used addicting chemicals. In the western culture the primary choice of drug has usually been alcohol. In Muslim countries, where the Koran has strictly forbidden the use of alcohol, marijuana has caused trouble for years. Similarly in Hindu countries the use of opium has been known since earliest history.

In the past few decades the social restraints on women drinking have been relaxed and the numbers of women drinking alcohol openly and socially has increased dramatically. Of course as more women drink, more women risk developing alcohol problems. Indeed the rate of increase in alcohol use among women has far surpassed the increase in the number of men drinking. Alcoholic beverage companies have not failed to observe this trend, resulting in increased advertising aimed at women and new products aimed specifically at the female market.

Research seems to indicate that the number of female alcoholics has also increased, with many researchers and clinicians believing that though the ratio of men and women entering Alcoholics Anonymous is now two-to-one, the more correct ratio is probably equal numbers of alcoholic men and women. The greater fear of exposure and social censure among women is the factor which stops them coming forward for help. This is borne out by the fact that many doctors and psychiatrists report one-to-one ratios of women to men alcoholics in their private practices. The fear and shame women have of admitting alcohol abuse and thus facing the possibility of social rejection, means that many women, even when they seek help, do not clearly state that their drinking is an issue. (They may have denied it to themselves so successfully that they firmly believe that their problems are not related to alcohol use.)

Many alcoholic women attend their doctor with problems of loneliness and anxiety, believing that there is a chemical solution to their unhappiness. Medical professionals sometimes attempt to pacify distress through drugs and this has resulted in approximately one quarter of alcoholic women also abusing prescribed drugs, primarily minor tranquillisers. Women are more likely than men to use alcohol in conjunction with other drugs. Women also tend to be much greater users of prescribed medications, particularly tranquillisers, even though they tend to figure less than men as users of illegal drugs such as heroin and cocaine.

The fact that many women use other drugs along with alcohol is an important issue if we are wondering about whether someone is alcoholic. Alcohol is just another drug, though it may be a more socially acceptable drug. It is important to look, not just at alcohol dependency, but also at an individual's overall chemical dependency. We need to examine just what the chemicals are which a woman is using to change her mood.

The need and desire to change mood is a common one. Unfortunately, the substances that have the power to change mood also have the power to cause addiction. Different drugs have a varying potential to addict; heroin, morphine, cocaine and designer drugs like crack have a high level of addictability, while other drugs like nicotine, marijuana and caffeine have a low addictability. If you have ever smoked tobacco you will remember it took some time and practice to become addicted; initially the experience is quite unpleasant but through determination (usually because of peer pressure) you persisted and eventually reached the stage that you felt you needed to smoke. This is called low addictability.

Because the addictive process is slow people sometimes believe that marijuana is not an addictive drug. But people do become dependent on marijuana and they feel they cannot get through a day without the drug.

Alcohol is located near the middle of an index of addictability, about halfway between heroin and caffeine. Almost anyone can become addicted to, or dependent upon, any of these mood-altering chemicals. If exposed to a high enough dose for a long enough period of time, addiction will occur. Addiction has two phases, psychological dependency and physical dependency. For most drugs psychological dependency precedes physical addiction. However, some of the new designer drugs on the street today seem to be physically addictive from the first experience of usage.

Psychological addiction

Psychological addiction is a learned behaviour. It is learned at the level of the autonomic nervous system rather than at the level of the central nervous system which incorporates the brain. The autonomic nervous system surrounds the spinal cord and connects the many nerves that run from the spine to the various organs of the body such as the heart, lungs and digestive system, controlling blood pressure, breathing, hormone production and cell metabolism. Also it connects to our sexual responses and bodily changes, which in turn affect our feelings, allowing us to experience sensations we identify as fear, anxiety or sexual stimulation.

Autonomic learning is the result of the strong feeling that accompanies the stimulation of our nerves. If we take a drug and we experience a pleasurable feeling then we are likely to repeat the drug to get the pleasurable feeling again. If a young woman with normal anxieties and fears is given a drug (alcohol) she will experience a 'high'. The world will seem good to her and she will feel good about herself, more relaxed, less nervous, more adequate. She will see things in a different light. The world will seem funny and her problems less intense. This is a positive experience and it is her first autonomic learning experience with a mood-altering chemical called ethanol.

If she repeats the experience frequently we may see a pattern developing where she copes more and more with her problems by using alcohol. She will have learned her lesson well. She will now be psychologically addicted or dependent on alcohol. An addict may be in trouble in every important area of her life but she will still go on using the drug. This is harmful psychological addiction.

It is not necessary to be physically addicted to be in trouble with chemicals and it is not necessary to experience a lot of organic changes to be in trouble with alcohol. When alcohol interferes in our well-being, or in the management of our social, family or work life and we still persist in using it, then we are psychologically addicted.

Physical addiction

If a woman is drinking consistently for a period of time certain changes that she is unaware of have been taking place in her body. When the time comes that she is physically ill if alcohol is withdrawn, then she is physically addicted or dependent. Physical addiction is relatively easy to treat and this aspect of an individual's dependency is dealt with during detoxification, either by her general practitioner as an outpatient, or while hospitalised. The process of detoxification is often called **drying out**. The physical part of the addiction is not a large problem and the individual can be withdrawn from alcohol in a short period of time while being kept fairly comfortable.

However, the woman is still left with the major problematic aspect of her addiction, her psychological dependency. If she thinks she is 'cured' because she has been physically withdrawn from alcohol, or if she believes she has dealt with her disease because she has stopped drinking, she will find recovery very difficult if not impossible. She needs support to tackle the psychological consequences of her disease.

Physical effects

What happens to the body when alcohol is drunk? And what happens when alcohol is drunk heavily and/or over a long period of time?

The human body is made up of millions of cells, each with a different job to do. Each different type of cell is called a tissue and has its own special use. A group of tissues may be combined to make up an organ in the body such as the heart or the liver. Each of the different tissues and organs in the human body works together in a systematic way and the organ depends on the work of the others. When we drink an alcoholic drink the alcohol passes into our blood stream mainly through the walls of the small intestine. The circulating blood brings the alcohol to the brain and the other organs and tissues.

Alcohol works directly on the brain and interferes with its ability to work. Let us look at oxygen deprivation as a parallel situation. A woman flying a small aeroplane without oxygen will experience physical changes as the plane rises because there is less and less oxygen in the air itself. The brain nerve tissue is particularly sensitive to this lack of oxygen and the brain suffers first and most. First her judgement becomes impaired because judgement depends on the highest brain centre and this is most sensitive to the lack of oxygen. Next, she becomes unable to govern the movement of her muscles in the way she wants. Her hands move awkwardly, her tongue and lips stumble as she tries to talk and she may sway or wobble as she tries to walk.

This lack of team-work by the muscles increases as the supply of oxygen becomes less and less. There is still enough oxygen for the muscle cells but the train which directs the organised, systematic team-work of the muscles is not getting enough. If the plane keeps rising eventually the woman will black out, she will become unconscious. If oxygen is restored, she will recover with a headache perhaps and an ill feeling. But if the plane rises further eventually even the brain centre which controls breathing will stop functioning, the heart cells will fail and she will die.

A similar pattern happens to a woman when she drinks alcohol. She will not be cut off from oxygen, but alcohol acts directly on the brain to disturb its ability to work, reaching more and more of the brain centres and shutting down more and more of the body's functions. Alcohol acts on the brain just like an anaesthetic. The more alcohol taken, the stronger the effect, that is, more of the brain is put to sleep.

It is important to realise that alcohol is a depressant drug. Sometimes we imagine alcohol as a stimulant, making us more lively so that we can be the life and soul of the party. Many women tell themselves that they are taking a drink to get them through their work, to liven themselves up, or to give them energy. Because alcohol is depressing the nervous system it *appears* to stimulate it. The lower centres of the brain relax their control, inhibitions are removed and there is a feeling of relaxation. This 'relaxation' is what leads to morning-after memories of 'I wish I hadn't said that!'

At the early stage of drinking alcohol, attention and judgement are impaired, as are self-discipline and fine skills of co-ordination. As the amount of alcohol consumed increases, our visual sense is impaired as is our capacity to recognise colour differences. Later, sensitivity to visual objects declines and loss or confusion of memory and errors in our co-ordination and balance occur. At this point we are intoxicated. The effect of alcohol is greater when the concentration in the brain is rising than when it is falling. It is particularly obvious when the rise is unusually quick as when a large amount of alcohol is drunk rapidly, particularly on an empty stomach. The amount of alcohol consumed is the primary factor determining how much alcohol is in the blood but there are other factors also determining the effects of alcohol on the body and these have significance for women.

Variable rate of absorption

Body build and weight affects the amount of alcohol carried in the blood. This is because the body tissues absorb alcohol. So the heavier an individual is, the lower the concentration of alcohol there is in the blood. However, fat will absorb only about one-fifth as much alcohol as will other body tissues. A woman's body, which is usually smaller and containing a higher proportion of fatty tissue than a man's, will reach an equal blood alcohol level to that of a man through consumption of less alcohol. In other words, women become drunk or intoxicated sooner.

The rate of absorption of alcohol into the blood stream is dependent on many factors. What you drink matters. It is generally agreed that distilled spirits such as whiskey, brandy, and gin, are absorbed more rapidly than wine or beer, leading to a higher maximum concentration of alcohol in the blood. The pace at which we drink is also significant due to the rate at which the body metabolises (burns up) the alcohol. For example, if wine is drunk slowly the body may be able to metabolise the alcohol almost as fast as it is absorbed, so the blood alcohol level remains low. However, if distilled spirits are drunk quickly the opposite occurs; the blood alcohol level remains high. The liver normally metabolises alcohol at a fixed rate (approximately one unit of alcohol per hour). Thus, if you drink more than one unit of alcohol per hour the alcohol builds up in the blood, leading to a higher blood-alcohol level. One unit of alcohol is the same as one half pint of beer, one glass of wine, one small sherry or one tot of spirits. (The tot is an English measure which contains .78 fluid ounces. By comparison, the Irish half glass or 'half one' of whiskey contains 1.25 fluid ounces.)

The ability of the liver to absorb alcohol can vary.

Frequent drinking increases the liver's metabolism. That means the liver can deal with alcohol more quickly. In time, however, with heavy drinking this ability becomes impaired and tolerance decreases. Also, a heavy drinker frequently absorbs alcohol more rapidly than a moderate drinker and so may reach a higher blood alcohol level with the same amount of alcohol.

The presence of food in the stomach can delay the absorption of alcohol into the blood, the extent of the delay depending largely on the fat content of the food. Blood alcohol levels do not return to normal as soon as drinking stops, but can remain high for some hours. This is why a person can still be drunk the next morning following a previous evening's drinking.

Research has shown that the blood alcohol level varies in women at different times in the menstrual cycle, the general trend is for women to become more intoxicated during their pre-menstrual time. Women on oral contraceptives or hormone replacement have been found to metabolise alcohol more slowly than other women. This may tie in with the fact that while pregnant, or where there are changes in the hormonal balance, women frequently describe changes in the physiological effects of alcohol. These descriptions mostly take the form of 'I couldn't tolerate as much alcohol', 'It made me feel sick', 'I feel sick after only a couple of drinks'.

So, when we drink, the immediate effects on our behaviour, mood and mental abilities is directly related to the level of alcohol in our blood.

Effects on the liver

Another factor determining how alcohol affects each individual is the efficiency and rate with which the liver metabolises the alcohol we have consumed. The liver is the organ in the body which breaks down alcohol into substances which are not harmful or toxic to our body. Alcohol abuse produces a whole range of cell damage in the liver, ranging from fatty liver, to alcoholic hepatitis, to cirrhosis. Women have been observed to develop cirrhotic problems and complications more readily than men do and to have a higher incidence of jaundice (hepatitis).

This vulnerability is of major concern. The liver is the largest organ in the body and has many important functions. Impaired liver function in the alcoholic contributes to the development of secondary complications: kidney failure, changes in blood chemistry and blood clotting, gastro-intestinal bleeding, brain disorders and ascites (an abnormal accumulation of fluid in the abdomen).

The first toxic effects of heavy alcohol consumption are the accumulation of large amounts of fat in the liver. The increased concentration of fat and resulting retention of protein and water in the liver cells causes the liver to become enlarged. This is known as fatty liver, and is a benign reversible condition, common in alcoholics. Abstinence from alcohol usually brings reversal of this damage. The presence of this condition usually indicates recent drinking.

Continued alcohol consumption can lead to widespread inflammation of the liver and destruction of hepatic tissue. This is known as hepatitis and a woman with this condition will suffer abdominal pain, fever and jaundice. This can progress to liver failure. The reversibility of alcoholic hepatitis depends on its severity. The liver will be scarred even if the alcoholic maintains complete abstinence.

Alcoholic cirrhosis is characterised by diffuse scarring of the liver. The progressive deterioration of the liver in cirrhosis due to chronic alcohol consumption can ultimately end in death from liver failure. Not every alcoholic develops cirrhosis so there may be a genetic factor such as a tendency towards liver vulnerability carried down through families. Studies have shown that the more alcohol a person consumes in a lifetime, the greater the likelihood of this person developing cirrhosis.

Effects on body muscles

Body muscles have also been shown to become weak and to degenerate due to chronic alcohol consumption. This damaging effect occurs not just in muscle throughout the body, but also in cardiac (heart) muscle. The heart is a muscular organ that can be damaged by chronic alcohol use. Heart strength is diminished significantly in alcoholics. Alcohol also affects heart size in a manner correlated to the total lifetime alcohol consumption. In other words, the more you drink, the more susceptible your heart becomes to damage. As the muscle fibres in the heart become damaged or die, the heart attempts to compensate for the injury by enlarging.

Effects on the brain

Excessive alcohol consumption can also seriously and sometimes irreversibly alter some of the activities of the brain, for example, memory and complex intellectual functioning. Indeed research has shown that even moderate levels of alcohol impair learning and memory capabilities. Alcohol is also now believed to be a factor in the cause of seizures and epileptic fits in chronic alcohol usage. Alcoholic beverages have long been associated with a role in triggering seizures. Seizures following intoxication are known as 'rum fits' or 'alcoholic epilepsy', as distinguished from primary epilepsy. Most scientists believe that withdrawal from alcohol rather than actual consumption is the prime culprit in alcohol-related seizures. However, seizures do occur as a direct effect of alcohol use. Alcohol use has also been shown to be injurious to select regions of the brain.

One of the surest signs of addiction to alcohol, or any drug, is an increased tolerance to it. A woman may pride herself on being able to 'drink her friends under the table', or in being able to 'keep partying all night long', without realising that this is damaging the brain and other cells. A heavy drinker often has the same blood alcohol level as a non-alcoholic but will show less signs of drunkenness. This is in part due to the fact that an alcoholic may have a much smaller concentration of alcohol in the brain than the non-alcoholic. Unfortunately as time progresses the increased tolerance to alcohol is lost and the alcoholic will soon be getting drunk with the same amount of alcohol as her non-alcoholic friend; later still she will get to the point where even a small amount of alcohol makes her drunk. This is because she is destroying brain cells at a rapid rate. Prolonged excessive alcohol intake can cause damage to the actual brain cells.

Withdrawal symptoms

There are other abnormal mental states caused by alcohol abuse, either as part of withdrawal symptoms or from vitamin deficiency.

Withdrawal symptoms can occur any time from a few hours to a few days after drinking has stopped. Milder symptoms begin earlier with the commonest state being acute tremulousness usually known as 'the shakes'. The most obvious feature is the gross shaking of the hands; indeed an alcoholic woman may be unable to dress herself or even hold a cup. People talk about this state when they say 'I need a drink to steady myself.' However, they are not talking about just physically steadying themselves. They often feel shaky inside too. Anxiety, physical restlessness and a feeling of weakness may accompany the tremors or may be the only symptoms. Depending on the amount of alcohol consumed, these shakes can last for as long as a week if more alcohol is not taken. If an individual is affected in this way she should seek medical supervision. Agitation and tremors may reach such an extent that she may not be able to sit still.

Alcohol has two major effects on brain function, sedation and increased activity. The sedative effect is rapid and usually leads to sleep. No one can get a sedative effect from any known drug without an agitating effect following. So, sedation of alcohol is naturally followed by agitation. Ultimately alcohol aggravates the alcoholic's physical state by further increasing both the severity and duration of hyperactivity. Eventually the sedation provided by the alcohol currently being consumed is inadequate to sedate the high cumulative level of hyperactivity. Also if she stops drinking, this hyperactivity will be revealed. She is then seen to have **withdrawal symptoms**. An alcoholic will continually try to medicate these symptoms not realising or understanding that when she drinks, she may be decreasing the shakes, the agitation and restlessness, but only temporarily. It is the alcohol which is causing the symptoms, she is not curing herself but making the situation worse.

Cross-addiction

Drugs known for their soporific (sleep inducing) effects such as librium, valium, equanil, soneryl, and tuinal have a prolonged sedative effect and offer the alcoholic temporary relief from discomfort. So cross-addiction to alcohol and one or more of the other sedatives is quite common. These sedatives are attractive to the alcoholic, allowing her to mask the effect of her activity and agitation. Alcohol has a sedative action for a shorter period of time than most of the other soporific drugs. This means that a coma resulting from an overdose of alcohol is rarely prolonged except when another sedative drug is being used.

The second most frequent cause of drug crises reported annually by hospital emergency units and crisis centres is alcohol taken in combination with other drugs. Statistics show that 90 per cent of drug overdoses involve women who are abusing *legal* substances such as alcohol or prescribed drugs. Forty-five per cent of such incidents involve alcohol in combination with another drug. Medical examiners' reports have indicated that tranquillisers are the third most common class of drugs reported as the cause of death. Forty-one per cent of such casualties are women.

The mixing of drugs is dangerous. One of the most

important findings from research in this area is that those who combine drug and alcohol abuse may be deceived as to the correctness of their judgements when taking these drugs. They are less able to judge the degree of their impairment from drinking alcohol if they have taken another drug. Indeed combining alcohol and, for example, valium increases intoxication without the woman being aware of the effect the alcohol may be producing. She, along with everyone else, may be mildly surprised to discover that she can pass out after only a 'few' drinks.

The abuse of other drugs in combination with alcohol is a serious problem for women in particular. Women are much more likely than men to try to medicate their feelings and their ills with any drug available to them. Polydrug abuse has increased among women. A 1977 study of Alcoholics Anonymous shows that 29 per cent of women were cross-addicted as opposed to 15 per cent of men. Of those members who were thirty years of age or younger, 55 per cent of women were cross-addicted and 36 per cent of men. Many women try to cope with loneliness, stress, anxiety and pressure by taking alcohol. They still remain under stress and therefore get sick a lot. They visit their doctor and get a prescription. But they do not listen to their doctor's warnings about drinking while taking prescribed drugs. They believe doctors say that about all drugs and that it doesn't mean very much. At the heart of this often unintentional drug-mixing is the failure to see alcohol as a drug, a potent, dangerous drug which can cause toxic reactions in all the organs of the body.

Delirium tremens

Delirium tremens is the dramatic consequence of very heavy drinking. Usually there has been at least ten years of excessive drinking before the first attack, which generally begins two to five days after stopping very heavy drinking.

Medical supervision of delirium tremens is essential. For the woman involved every conscious moment is one of extreme fear. She is very restless and agitated, never still, tossing and turning, constantly engaged in conversation, switching from person to person, subject to subject every moment. Fear, agitation and great distraction are the dominant features. She is also subject to ever-changing visual hallucinations usually of a threatening nature such as being attacked by objects or animals. She is completely disorientated, may not know where she is, the date or even the month. She is intensely suggestible and will respond to suggestions and promptings. In her confused state she acts on fears and suspicions which she normally represses.

Unchecked, the condition usually takes three or four days to run its course, but the more subtle aspects may take weeks to subside. Some anxiety, insomnia and a shortened span of attention may persist for two weeks or longer after the condition is apparently over.

Delirium tremens is a withdrawal reaction. The greater the alcohol consumption and the longer the length of the drinking bout the more delayed the appearance of the symptoms. It can be dangerous unless modified by drugs. At one time, when drunk men were thrown into the 'cooler' or prison cell to calm down, 15-20 per cent of individuals with this degree of toxicity would die without medical attention. It is important to recognise the necessity of having a woman medically supervised if she intends to stop drinking.

Vitamin deficiency

Certain syndromes resulting from chronic alcoholism are largely irreversible. Korsakov's syndrome is due to a deficiency in vitamin B, causing a severe disturbance of memory. The woman's awareness is not affected, there is no confusion, but there is selective memory loss. It is unbelievable how short-lived the memory can be in such a situation. One woman awoke each morning believing she had been admitted to hospital the previous night. Another woman did not recognise people and experienced each meeting as the first. To compensate for the memory loss the sufferer will make up stories and invent circumstances to fill the gaps.

In another condition, Wennincke's Encephalopathy, there is difficulty in concentrating and in answering questions, though the woman may be very aware. Often, but not always, there is some memory loss. There is frequently a disturbance in gait and balance. This condition is also due to deficiency of vitamin B and is related to changes in particular areas in the base of the brain.

Individuals drinking large quantities of alcohol often suffer from vitamin deficiency. Small amounts of alcohol increase the secretions which aid digestion (this is why people often take an aperitif before meals). However, large amounts of alcohol cause loss of appetite, disturbed digestion, impaired absorption of food, and vomiting. In chronic cases individuals are found to have serious nutritional deficiencies because although alcohol supplies calories it contains no vitamins, proteins or minerals.

Any type of vitamin deficiency can occur when a woman is drinking heavily and failing to eat properly. However, the most characteristic deficiencies are those associated with vitamin B depletion. The symptons often begin with numbness and weakness in the feet, moving upwards. This condition may begin at the fingertips and work upwards. This may seriously impair a woman's ability to walk. She may find it impossible to step in the dark when she cannot see where she is placing her feet. These symptoms are largely correctable by vitamin replacement therapy in large doses.

Effects on nerve cells

Peripheral neuropathy is another syndrome frequently associated with chronic alcoholism. Alcohol alone can cause damage to the nerve cells but poor nutrition results in deficiencies which aggravate the condition. The woman will experience tingling and the recovery is slow and uncertain.

Effects on the stomach

In a woman with ulcers the added flow of juices in the stomach is harmful. Heartburn is often experienced when alcohol is drunk on an empty stomach; this is due to the irritation of the stomach lining by the acid. Some heavy drinkers have a chronic inflammation of the lining of the stomach. Gastritis and ulceration of the stomach may require surgical intervention.

Effects on the kidneys

Alcohol does not have a direct effect on the kidneys. Rather it affects the pituitary gland which is a small extension of the lower part of the brain. One of the substances the pituitary gland releases into the blood stream controls the formation of urine. As alcohol reduces the activity of this gland the kidneys form more urine.

Effects on the pancreas

Chronic pancreatitis is an irreversible disorder which is linked to alcoholism. The pancreas secretes insulin and aids the regulation of blood sugar levels in the body. Disorders of this level can be fatal. Pancreatitis, as well as causing disorders of blood sugar levels, causes malabsorption of proteins and fats. Persistent drinking with this condition can be fatal.

Hypothermia

Alcohol increases the flow of blood in vessels near the skin. Because more blood reaches the skin, the person feels warm. In fact, the increased flow of blood to the skin means that the person is losing heat. Hypothermia is a danger one and a half to two hours after drinking begins.

Effects on reproductive cycle

Alcohol has an adverse effect on the reproductive capability in both men and women. The reproductive function may be impaired through the direct or indirect effects of alcohol abuse. Studies show that alcohol damages cells of the testes, causing diminished production of testosterone in men. This is commonly detected as diminished levels of testosterone (male sex hormone) and elevated levels of oestrogen (female sex hormone) in alcoholic men with liver disease. Failure of the reproductive function in men is often manifested as decreased sperm production, testicular atrophy and loss of secondary sex characteristics. These alcohol-induced disorders result from decreased circulating testosterone.

The majority of medical doctors and psychologists recommend that women don't drink at all during pregnancy. This is because evidence gathered from studies on the consequences of maternal alcohol use on the foetus clearly indicates that alcohol can cause birth defects and behavioural problems in babies of women who consume alcohol while pregnant. Indeed prenatal alcohol exposure is one of the leading known causes of mental retardation in the western world. Problems with learning, attention, memory and problem solving are common, along with uncoordination, impulsiveness and speech and hearing defects. Defects in learning skills persist even into adolescence and adulthood.

The impact of alcohol on the brain of the developing foetus can cause life-long problems of social adjustment. Low self-esteem, isolation, loneliness, depression, immaturity, stubbornness, inappropriate sexual behaviour, hostility, abusiveness, even violence, are symptoms of pre-natal alcohol exposure. There are degrees of adverse effects with defects occurring even where the mother drank moderately. Where mothers drink an average of more than three ounces of alcohol (six drinks) per day during early pregnancy, one fully developed case of FAS (Foetal Alcohol Syndrome) per 100 women occurs. This is preventable.

• • •

Women are more at risk physically from alcohol than men. Their size and build and biological make-up leaves them more vulnerable to the toxic consequences of consuming alcohol. Cultural mores and attitudes against women getting drunk means that women are put at further risk because they do not seek help for their alcoholism. Instead they hide their drinking and deny their addiction, retreating into isolation, helplessness and illness as masking devices. They frequently substitute other sedatives for alcohol in an attempt to deal with their addiction and to find a chemical answer to their ever-increasing anxiety in a form more acceptable to themselves and to society.

No matter which sedative they are using they are applying a chemical hammer on their brain cells. Ethyl alcohol stops the brain cells from working temporarily and of course this can be pleasurable. However, if the drinker takes enough ethyl alcohol she can kill the nerves.

Effects on the brain take place in 100 per cent of alcoholics. These descriptions of how alcohol affects a woman's body is an essential element in grasping the full picture of how alcoholism affects the individual. When a woman becomes alcohol dependent she becomes affected not just in certain areas of her life, but in every aspect of herself. She becomes affected intellectually, emotionally and physically. All her powers become both distorted by and focused on alcohol. In the physical realm, she is not just endangered when the symptoms become full blown and unavoidable, as for example, cirrhosis of the liver. Rather the alcohol is affecting and distorting her internal environment gradually and insidiously in a progressive way. She is not necessarily aware of the physical changes in her body and how she is being damaged, but they are nonetheless present and altering her well-being.

• • •

SUSAN

Susan (the mother of three children who drinks at home) certainly doesn't connect her lack of energy, her feelings of fatigue, edginess and depression with her drinking. She is sleeping less and less well, often waking around four or five o'clock in the morning, clammy and sick, with a growing sense of unease and fear. She puts this down to 'nerves' and goes to her local GP with problems of sleeplessness and anxiety. She fails to tell him about her drinking, focusing rather on the family money problems, her need to work and the pressure she is under. She leaves the surgery happy, with her prescription for valium safely in her bag. She feels much safer, unaware that her problems are now compounded, just as her GP is unaware that Susan has just begun a journey to cross-addiction and has found a source to supply her habit.

Susan doesn't realise that her feelings of sluggishness, tiredness, anxiety and depression are related directly to her deteriorating physical condition. Her drinking is taking its toll on the major organs of her body, her heart, liver, pancreas and muscles. They are not functioning as efficiently as before and she is becoming progressively weaker and less able to handle the demands of her everyday life. She hasn't made the connection between her difficulty in sleeping through the night, her night sweats and her drinking habits. Neither is she aware of the damage the alcohol is doing to her stomach when she drinks rather than eats. She has been suffering a lot with indigestion and acidy heartburn and eats antacids and mints constantly. Because of this discomfort she often chooses not to eat; she doesn't feel hungry. She drinks to 'give her energy'. Of course the food she eats does not supply her with sufficient vitamins and minerals, added to which her body is unable to absorb the vitamins and minerals she does take in.

The lack of vitamin B and calcium in particular causes Susan problems at present and will in the future. Her skin is becoming dry and more wrinkled due to the effect of alcohol. Her drinking is creating a time bomb in her body, a time bomb waiting to explode in one of or several areas at any time. The effect of alcohol on her health in general means that Susan feels constantly run-down and lacking in energy. She takes no exercise and in fact now gets breathless after climbing a few steps. She is becoming aware that she can't think her way through a problem the way she used to and that her memory isn't quite there. That this may be largely due to the effects of ethyl alcohol on her nervous system is not a conscious issue for Susan. How long these brain injuries will remain reversible is unclear, but unless she receives help in the form of clear acknowledgement that alcoholism is a destructive factor in her life, she is at risk of becoming permanently disabled. The likelihood of permanent disablilty is greater because this alcoholic is a woman.

Chapter Five
The preoccupation with alcohol

PAT

If we were to ask Pat on any particular day what was the first thing she thought of that morning, her answer would, invariably be drink. Her first waking thought after a probably disturbed and restless night is about that which is most important to her. Her last thought at night before she goes to sleep is the same, drink. Of course Pat would not readily admit this, if she would admit it at all. She does not let anyone into her own private, personal world of alcohol. Others may guess or suspect how she is, but Pat protects and guards the true nature of her way of life from everyone. 'People don't like me anyway and if they really knew what I'm like, and what I do, they'd hate me,' she thinks to herself. 'I don't need them anyway. They think I'm crazy and so I am. They think I'm stupid and they would love an opportunity to laugh at me and make a fool of me. I'd die if they knew, if they found out.'

An isolated life
So Pat keeps herself to herself. Isolated from the people around her, she lives mostly in the bedroom of her flat, keeping the blinds lowered so that no one can peer in without effort. Usually she doesn't answer the door, not even to casual callers. She jumps with fright at the slightest

sound. The idea of visitors terrifies her, feeling as she does. She does not feel capable of negotiating the simplest communication with other people. Indeed she disconnected the doorbell because she found its ringing so alarming. If someone calls to the door she peeks out her bedroom door and anxiously waits for them to go away.

Pat lives every day full of fear, anxious about every possible problem and every possible occurrence. Will the cat next-door knock over the milk bottle? Will she have enough hot water to do the washing? Will the stain come off the sheets? The most overwhelming fear is, will she be able to get a drink today?

Tuesday is a good day, because today she gets her welfare cheque and that means she is sure of a drink. On a day when there is no money for drink and nothing left in her collection of bottles, Pat resorts to sleeping tablets. She tries to sleep her way through the day. On the days when she has neither, Pat has a very hard time. She is bad tempered, angry, grumpy and despairing. When neighbours meet her on the road, she keeps her head down and mutters 'Good day' under her breath. She doesn't want them to look at her even, and definitely not to talk to her. At the same time she feels constantly scrutinised, often turning around because she feels eyes upon her. She is not surprised when there is no one there. 'Where did they go?' she wonders. Her paranoia and suspicions are so real to her that she doesn't doubt her own reactions.

Neighbours wonder and worry as they observe Pat but any attempts to approach her or to offer her even the most basic civilities are rebuffed and rejected so definitely that it is easier for everyone concerned to merely tolerate and even ignore her. Her appearance is becoming more and more unkempt and scruffy. She cuts her own hair rather than go to a hairdresser. Her once stylish and neat hairstyle is now shapeless and greying. She is no longer interested in colouring her hair. She would not spend the money she needs for drink on her image. She doesn't spend money on clothes either. Sometimes she intends to but the desire for a bottle always diverts her in the direction of the off-licence or the supermarket. Her clothes are the same ones she has worn for years. Frequently she sleeps in them.

On days when Pat has not yet had a drink, she can manoeuvre her way to her destination quickly and without interference. However, some days she has already found solace in drink before she leaves the house and her gait is awkward and even stumbling. On these days her manner is different; she is apologetic and even talkative. Her conversation is always the same, however. It invariably comes around to the subject of marriage and husbands, in particular her husband. Pat isn't happy about her husband and her husband's behaviour even after all these years. When she has a good few drinks on her she is quite willing to share her views with anyone who will listen. In fact, if allowed or encouraged, she will express them quite vehemently, even crudely. She will even repeat them if given enough time. These occasions occur infrequently and Pat would deny they ever happen. Partly this is due to the fact that she so frequently has blackouts, when she doesn't remember what she said or did. Her brain is damaged by alcohol and during this state she is not really conscious of what she is saying; her awareness is clouded.

Drink, the only hope

Pat's way of life is drink-centred. But her internal mental and emotional state is also drink-centred. Alcohol is affecting her physically, mentally and emotionally, and she experiences these changes as distressing and frightening. She is troubled by vague fears and anxieties. She feels edgy and unsettled, physically shaky and trembling, with a sense of foreboding and imminent disaster always present. She has deep, dark, black moods and a sense of loathing and self-hatred. She dislikes herself, dislikes her body and believes herself to be a failure, a 'waste of space'. She is angry also with her family, her husband, and her friends, whom she thinks have misunderstood her over the years and treated her unfairly. Life, all in all, has dealt her a bad hand, she believes, and she feels powerless to retaliate or to direct or change the future. She thinks of herself as a hopeless case, a woman who couldn't even have children. Her only hope, as she sees it, is her drink.

Alcohol provides an escape, an answer, a way out from the ceaseless merry-go-round of bad health and negative feelings. What Pat is unaware of and is unable to see, is that alcohol has created these experiences and feelings. Over the years she restructured and re-orientated not only her way of life but also her attitudes and recall of past events to accommodate her dependency on alcohol. At this point the miseries of loneliness, anxiety, depression, hatred, resentment and remorse have driven her to despair. Her lifestyle now requires alcohol to wipe out all feelings. She is drinking to oblivion. Pat's life is now a living death, the ante-chamber of total and final self-destruction.

A broken marriage

Over the years as Pat's personal and social life revolved more and more around her desire to drink, as she chose to go places, do things and be with people in accordance with whether they fitted in with her drinking or not, as she avoided situations and people which threatened her drinking, she learned to evaluate and judge what was most important to her happiness in relation to her sick need for alcohol. She developed anger, aversion, hatred and blame towards those people who questioned her drinking or her drinking behaviour. She became more and more hostile towards anyone who would not conform to the conditions set by her alcoholism.

Her husband was one person Pat was not prepared to listen to. His feelings and thoughts about the way she was living her life threatened her totally. She did not want him to question her drinking, she did not connect her bad form and angry moods with her alcohol intake and instead she rationalised her marital difficulties by blaming her husband. He was being unfair, expecting too much; what about *his* moods and demands. Rather than give up the alcohol, she gave up her marriage. Pat would deny this. To her mind the marriage broke up because she couldn't have children. Pat firmly believes that her husband walked away because of this, that he didn't really love her but only wanted a family.

For Tom, Pat's husband, the reality had been quite different. For a long time he begged, pleaded, threatened and cajoled her in an effort to get her to stop drinking. One day he hit her. That was the day he walked away from the marriage forever. Like many husbands of alcoholic women he left home, never having told anyone of the problems alcohol was causing.

First thought of the day

That the first thing Pat thinks about in the morning is alcohol would not be surprising to the thousands of alcoholic women in this country. Most addicted individuals, if they were being honest with themselves, would admit that they can identify with this. To be obsessed with alcohol is part and parcel of alcohol dependency. It works like the tune you hear on the radio that insists on replaying inside your head all day. You don't consciously invite it, but it keeps repeating itself despite your efforts to banish it.

We can all become obsessed especially when we feel hurt or unfairly treated. Resentment can build up and though we tell ourselves, 'It's over and done with, forget it', emotions, thoughts and fantasies can be stirred up time and time again in spite of our best efforts. The preoccupation with alcohol that is part of the addiction is like this. It is largely subconscious and hidden from the alcoholic woman's awareness. Her defences confuse her thinking and she protects herself from full awareness. She is not only focused on drink but absorbed by it. All her mental processes, memory, intellect, imagination are involved. She knows some element of her preoccupation and this convinces her that she is quite reasonable and aware of her involvement with alcohol. However, she has no way of knowing that her relationship with alcohol is quite irrational. She is not able to recognise the way she is distorting the reality of what is happening. She is preoccupied with getting drunk, with having money for drink, with the unwelcome and unexpected consequences of getting drunk, with other people's reactions, with blackouts and confused memories, with covering up her mistakes, with pretending everything is fine, with the mounting guilt, anxiety and remorse.

More and more she needs relief from this pressing mental burden of worry. 'My head is spinning'; 'I don't know where my head is'; 'My mind is racing'; the alcoholic woman will complain as her lack of concentration becomes obvious. Ultimately she tells herself, 'If they had my problems, they'd drink too.'

All her mental powers are drawn into supporting her relationship with alcohol. Alcoholics show tremendous creativity in hiding their drink, in inventing ways of getting it, in misleading and deceiving those who would interfere.

But the woman obsessed with alcohol is not available for communication. She is too distracted to give proper attention to others. This is why an alcoholic is 'out of it' even when not drinking. She cannot concentrate on the business at hand. She forgets appointments, burns dinners, doesn't listen to her friends. Her obsession can be transferred to secondary issues also. For example, the woman who is obsessed with her sexual behaviour and feels guilty may go to a clergyman for help. If he focuses on her morality to the exclusion of her alcoholism, he will add to her distress because she is not in control of this behaviour when drunk. Similarly a doctor may diagnose physical problems as a primary concern because of a woman's preoccupation with them, without realising *they* are the complications of alcohol dependency.

This is why it is so easy for Pat and many women like

her to get other drugs prescribed for them. A medical doctor may believe that she is drinking to get to sleep, or to cope with anxiety, if he is aware of the drinking at all. Again if a woman is preoccupied with marital or family problems, a social worker or counsellor may conclude that these problems are the main issue. For Pat this has led to people excusing her drinking and turning a blind eye to it on the basis that she drinks because of the breakdown of her marriage.

SUSAN

Susan shows great creativity when it comes to hiding her drink and preventing Ed from knowing she is drinking. She now goes to great lengths to hide her bottles. This is because Ed has started to take a stand about her alcohol consumption, mostly by pouring any drink he finds down the sink. He has at least admitted to himself that Susan's moods, her anger, and her now regular unconsciousness at night is due to drinking rather than to tiredness or overwork.

Because of Ed's adeptness at finding her hiding places and the frequency with which her beloved alcohol disappears, Susan has begun to hide several bottles at a time. Initially a boot in the wardrobe was her hiding place. When that was found she moved to the laundry basket. Then it was in the garage in various nooks and crannies. She'd hide bottles under the children's beds, under her own mattress, under the stairs. She'd fill small lemonade bottles and put them in the pockets of coats. She'd place bottles in the cistern of the toilet, in empty saucepans, in the casserole dishes.

Frequently she'd place bottles among the clothes piled for ironing or among the dirty clothes in the washing machine. She stopped that the day her thirteen-year-old daughter Tracey needed a blouse washed for her youth club and put the machine on to wash. When Tracey came back she found her mother sitting on the kitchen floor, crying, looking at the washing spinning around in the machine. Susan convinced Tracey that she had slipped and banged her elbow and that despite her tears she was fine. She sat on the floor, however, until the wash cycle finished, praying that the bottle would not break. She wept not because she was worried about glass getting into Tracey's blouse and the other clothes, but because she feared that her precious liquid would be lost. Susan did not allow herself to see the insanity and irrationality of her behaviour. Instead she decided she wouldn't hide her alcohol there again.

When Ed went up the stairs Susan got into a panic until he came down again, fearful that he might have found her precious cache. On the occasions when he did find a bottle, she watched him pour it down the sink and promised herself another bottle the next day. Or else she consoled herself, knowing that she had hidden another bottle elsewhere.

Susan bought her alcohol at the large neighbourhood supermarket so that she could hide it among the groceries. Usually she did her shopping on a Wednesday night because she knew that between 6 pm and 9 pm the supermarket reduced the price of drink. One night, coming back from shopping, she saw Ed's car parked outside the house. She hid her bottles over a wall. She spent the evening sick with the thought that someone would find them, and wished fervently that Ed would go out. She had one special spot behind a bush near the side gate of the house. After going to the off-licence or supermarket Susan would go round the back, hide the bottle by the bush, then go around the front and check there was no one in the house.

The compulsion to drink

Susan never allowed herself to believe that the children

knew she was drinking. She always drank either a quick gulp straight from the hidden bottle or else she drank from a mug. She never drank from a glass, even when alone, as if somehow pretending even to herself that it was coffee, lemonade or milk she was drinking, not alcohol. She couldn't relax and have a drink in an easy, natural way even when there was no one to observe her. She would fill a mug and drink it as she moved around the house, barely tasting it. The mug would be emptied in a flash, too quickly, and she would go back to fill it, telling herself that this time she would enjoy it. Susan was unable to drink normally even when she had no one to hide from. Her anxiety was too high, her compulsion too strong. She constantly told herself she would only have one, or two, but she always drank more. Recently, when out socially, or in a family member's home, if she could only have one or two drinks she'd prefer to have none. Even when pressed to have a drink, Susan would refuse, hoping people would think she was great and also because the thought of not having enough to drink was more than she could bear.

Susan's compulsion to drink, like that of other alcoholics, is largely subconscious. If she was asked about it she would sincerely deny it. Susan believes with fervent conviction that she knows about her relationship with alcohol. She sincerely believes that she could stop drinking if she wanted to, that she can 'take it or leave it', that she still has control over her drinking. She is sincerely deluded about the hold that alcoholism has over her and how it is dominating her life. She has acquired an urge or compulsion to drink, an impulsive emotive craving which keeps her addiction, her alcohol dependency, right on course.

• • •

Our emotions work hand-in-hand with our mind and intellect. When we recall and fantasise and think about good experiences we have a corresponding feeling in our gut. Similarly, when an individual has alcohol-induced good feeling, her head is busy taking notes about it. She can then recall and fantasise and think about those alcohol experiences, and her thoughts bring with them emotional inclinations. As her reflections and preoccupations become more frequent and more intense, her feelings for alcohol grow more urgent. These feelings of urgency in turn stimulate further preoccupation. So, the alcohol dependent woman is trapped on a merry-go-round of obsession and compulsion. This, because it is acquired, is a reversible cycle. Treatment can help remove the mental obsession with alcohol and the emotional disorder that accompanies it.

The women we meet in this book have become dependent on a mood-altering chemical. They have come to rely on alcohol to change their mood and feeling and inevitably to medicate the distress, disquiet and anxiety the alcohol itself perpetrates. They now equate any change in feeling or emotion with a desire to drink. Changes in mood, both up and down, for the alcoholic, lead to thoughts of alcohol. The more a woman relies on alcohol for changes of feelings, the more her emotional life becomes stunted. The euphoria after a drink is great while it lasts, and it only lasts for shorter and shorter periods, but it is always followed by a downward move into discomfort and misery.

For the alcoholic, the highs are increasingly not so high and the lows are increasingly lower. Eventually to be depressed and low is the norm. the alcoholic woman now drinks just to cope with her misery. She needs to drink.

LINDA

During work Linda (single career woman) plans how she will go out that night to drink. She tells herself she is planning her social life and to the extent that she has no social activities that don't involve drink, that is true. She plays badminton and goes bowling and plays football. However, she drinks before most of these activities and always after. Increasingly she finds it difficult to concentrate on work, particularly after a session the night before. On those days Linda feels in the depths, full of fear and self-hatred. She wakes up in the morning wondering what is going to go wrong that day and when in work thinks people are talking about her and disliking her. On mornings like this Linda tries to avoid people as much as possible, only speaking when it is essential. She can see work isn't developing as it should but rationalises this, blaming the firm, the market and her position.

When she goes out to a venue at night she tries to make sure she arrives first and has a few drinks before her companions arrive. When ordering a drink Linda goes to the counter and buys herself a double, hiding the fact by pouring her lemonade into the glass before going back to the table. On other occasions she'll buy her friend a double also, to ensure that she gets as drunk and doesn't notice Linda's drinking. When the bar closes and others are chatting, Linda is obsessed with going on to a disco, simply to get more alcohol. Regardless of how long she has been drinking, regardless of whether she has been home that night or not, Linda always intends to go to a disco or nightclub. If her companions don't decide quickly enough, she goes to the nightclub on her own. She is well known there; she is one of the regulars and likes to think of herself as one of the *élite*. Her tolerance of alcohol is high, at this stage in her drinking, which enables her to deny her obvious preoccupation with alcohol. Instead she tells herself she is a socialite who thrives on the high life. Because of her high tolerance to alcohol, she never hesitates about driving home. She tells herself she is a good driver and that she isn't drunk, no matter how many drinks she has had that night.

Creating a prison

It is now normal for Linda to live in this manner. She does not recognise the fact that her drinking is out of control. She is partly aware of the things she does not like about her drinking, but the only way she has to relieve this guilt is to drink more. Alcohol is taking charge of her life, her thoughts, her feelings, her attitudes to hobbies, friends and work. Compulsion to drink is in the driver's seat in her life, urging her toward alcohol. Similarly she is being repelled away from any people or situations that threaten her relationship with alcohol. She finds people who drink less, or who drink less often, boring and staid. She avoids occasions and situations where alcohol is not available, preferring to choose those places where she can drink unnoticed.

Linda is like the pony tethered to a pole with a long rope. Over the course of time, and by constantly circling the pole, he winds the rope around and around the pole. The circle is getting smaller and smaller, though the pony is so busy chomping he fails to notice. So it is for Linda. She is so busy, preoccupied with drinking, that she cannot see beyond alcohol. She cannot see the prison she is creating for herself, the contracting circle of her life.

Chapter Six
Personality changes:
How alcohol affects the way we behave

SUSAN

The pattern of Susan's life has changed dramatically. Her life can now be divided into the days when she is drinking and the days when she is not. When she is drinking her mood is hyper. When she is not drinking she is in the depths of depression. She is full of fear and hatred about what she is doing to her health and to her family. Her days are one long lie.

Susan now finds it impossible to be honest about what is really going on, either to herself or to others. She cannot think straight or trust people, even her best friends. She feels that people are out to get her, that people are talking about her and that they hate her. She avoids everyone and will not talk to anyone unless she has to. Susan is powerless to resist alcohol. It has taken over her life. Alcohol now dictates how her time is spent, what she does, who she spends her day with, what her mood is. It also affects her thinking, how she feels and how she reacts to all the people in her life, from the postman or the butcher to her friends, her husband and her children.

No matter what promises she makes to herself or to Ed, alcohol continues to take over. It rules her thoughts and actions. She would go to any lengths to get a drink, regardless of who gets hurt in the process. Susan has never tried to quit drinking because she does not see drinking as the problem. Instead, she believes she has no discipline, that she needs to get her life in order, change her way of life in order to be happy. On her bad days she believes she needs to change everything, her friends, her house, her children, her husband, her body, her face, even the dog. If these things were different, she'd be okay, she thinks. She feels angry at the world because she feels so bad inside; she kicks the chairs because they keep getting in her way, she hates the carpets because they keep getting dirty; she loathes the children because they demand her time and energy; she keeps the dog locked out the back because she cannot bear the way he looks at her.

Money problems

Money is always a problem. There is never enough. This is the only level at which Susan attempts to control her drinking. She becomes determined to drink only a certain quantity at a time. She brings only the exact amount of money to the supermarket, or she goes to the small shop on the corner instead, so she cannot buy alcohol. However, she never succeeds in keeping these promises to herself. Time and time again she comes home from the supermarket with a small bottle of vodka and no disinfectant/washing powder/ketchup. She intends to walk to the small shop but instead goes straight on to the off-licence down the street.

Susan ends up short of money for house-keeping. She has started to borrow money. She lies to her sister Joan about the financial situation at home, hinting at difficulties Ed is experiencing in the job, moaning about how hard-up she is, how she can't afford this or that. Joan is a soft touch, an easy-going woman who becomes embarrassed at the thought of Susan's financial difficulties. She has no children of her own and feels guilty about her abundance of worldly goods when faced with the plea in Susan's voice. Money is quietly shoved into Susan's pocket at the end of a visit. Joan will never ask for repayment.

Afraid of reality

Susan's attempts to cut down on her drinking fail. They fail because when she isn't drinking she feels worse, more depressed than ever. She does not really want to live her life in reality, in the harsh light of an alcohol-free day. These failures to keep the promises she makes to herself cause her guilt, uneasiness and conflict, despite all her best efforts. She denies the reality of her alcoholism in many ways. She minimises the exact amount of alcohol she is consuming, in her conversation with others. She lies to Ed when he asks if she is drinking or how much she has drunk. She'll deny it if she can get away with it, replying 'No! Definitely not', 'No, not a drop', when he demands to know how much she's drinking. Her lies are so important to her she nearly believes them herself. She gets angry and hurt when the question of drinking is raised, despite the fact that she has been sipping all day from the large bottle of vodka hidden safely away. Ed does not know about the money she is borrowing, or the fact that Thomas their son did not need thirty pounds for his computer course in school. Susan fabricates reasons to explain the amount of money she is withdrawing from their account each week.

When Susan fails to control her drinking she distracts herself by getting angry at those around her. She quarrels with Ed about how little he is earning and the difficulty of managing a household and feeding the family with the money she has available. She blames Ed for the shortages in the home, rather than question the amount she is drinking. Despite her efforts to conceal from herself her failure to control her drinking, Susan's disappointment and discouragement is increasing daily. She dislikes herself more and more.

Husband and children

Ed also is increasingly frustrated. He is increasingly aware of the problem and is also attempting to control Susan's drinking. He does this by challenging and questioning her about her drinking, by searching for bottles of alcohol around the house, by pouring any alcohol he finds down the sink. Ed is watching Susan all the time. He knows her every move and will recognise if she has been drinking the minute he looks at her or hears her voice. He tries to reason with her and bargains about when she can drink and how much. He extracts promises from her. Susan promises not to drink before the children are in bed, not to drink more than two small glasses of vodka, to drink only at weekends, not to drink in the bedroom or kitchen, not to buy alcohol herself, only to drink with Ed. Of course she does not keep any of these promises. Instead she increases her dishonesty and lies, making excuses, sneaking drink, even stealing from Ed's pocket. All attempts to control the drinking fail.

These failures, coupled with frequent drunken episodes, cause Susan to suffer guilt, shame and fear. Despite the promises, Ed knows what he will find on returning home. Somedays everything looks fine, Susan is busy with the children, the dinner is ready and she will talk to him about the events of the day. On other occasions the house will seem to be functioning normally, but he can detect the slur in her voice, see the curved slope of her shoulders that betrays her intoxication. Those are disappointing days for Ed.

But the worst days are the ones when he returns home to find Susan very drunk. On those days she is slumped in front of the television, or asleep on the sofa or in bed. Or, for that again, she could be shouting at the children, banging pots in the kitchen or sitting at the kitchen table crying copiously. On such a day the children are like ghosts about the house, gliding white-faced and silent up to their rooms or escaping out to their friends' homes. The next day Susan will be knotted with guilt and anxiety, expressing remorse and guilt, tearful and full of embarrassment at her drunkenness. She will be apologetic, making promises not to do it again, to change for the better. Ed is now familiar with her pleading for sympathy and understanding, her acknowledgements that she is 'not perfect; no one is'. For a day she overcompensates with all the family, being overly affectionate and overly indulgent with the children. After a drunken episode Ed now knows that Susan will initiate sex, attempting to appease him and to overcome her own feelings of worthlessness.

• • •

This pattern of thwarted attempts to control the drinking, followed by the alcoholic's increased self-loathing and the increased frustration and anger of her family and friends, reflects the lack of recognition of the progression of the illness by all involved. There is a failure to realise that the alcoholic woman is 'out of control' and that she is powerless with alcohol. She can no longer decide rationally, or act logically or responsibly towards alcohol. In her attempts to deny this powerlessness she ends up lying, cheating, scheming and conning all those who are close to her. Her partner, family members and friends fail to grasp the extent to which the disease has gripped her.

The changes in the personality of an alcoholic are noticed and commented upon. People are aware of these changes, but frequently onlookers do not connect these apparent attitude problems with the individual's drinking. Alcohol dependent women become increasingly negative in their outlook on life.

LINDA

Linda's family and friends notice a deterioration in her frame of mind. Usually a cheerful, bouncy, energetic young woman, she has become quiet and distant. She no longer freely chats to everyone and anyone. Instead she looks dull and withdrawn, preoccupied with her own issues and disinterested in her family and friends. Once optimistic and enthusiastic about her work, a sour note has crept in to her comments about her employers, her salary, her prospects and her workmates. Hopelessness seems to permeate her attitude towards the future and her parents worry about her gloomy thinking. She has become judgemental, frequently running down and criticising her younger brothers and sisters, complaining about politics, religion, the church, the community and the world in general.

No one realises that Linda is projecting her own failures and weaknesses onto others. She is increasingly doubtful about herself and her abilities, full of anxiety and worry about herself. She suspects there is something wrong with her, that she might have deep mental or emotional problems, but she cannot put her finger on what it is. Meanwhile she deals with these feelings by drinking!

Linda is full of suspicion. She is not sure what she is suspicious of, but she feels uncertain and unsure of herself and others most of the time. The development of her pattern of sneaking drinks, playing down the amounts she is drinking, lying to her family about where she is at night, lying in work about her absences and deficits in her work quota, all contribute in a real way to creating the suspicion that others disapprove of her and want to interfere. This is probably true. They do, but they don't know what to do.

Linda experiences other people's concern for her as persecution and becomes even more furtive and withdrawn. She now always 'expects the worst'.

PAT

Pat has retreated further and further into her own world. She is entrenched in loneliness. In avoiding people, she rejects them and cuts herself off from them. She is now left all alone, isolated, rejected, lonely and desolate. Over the years people have tried to connect with her; her brother in particular has really tried. Eventually everyone has stopped trying. Her aversion to their company, her dislike of visits, conversations, any contact, all became quite tangible. She wouldn't answer the door; she would hang up on telephone conversations; she would walk past people on the street; pretend she had fallen asleep when they were talking to her. Anything and everything to avoid them.

Of course people believed that Pat was avoiding them and their company, but the issue that was really dangerous for Pat was any imagined or implied threat to her drinking. By avoiding relationships she warded off any possible dangers to her addiction. This is not a conscious process and Pat would not have much insight into her feelings or her behaviour. The aversion she has to company has become real for her. She does not connect it to her drinking any more than her family and friends do.

SUSAN

Susan has also changed. Her family and friends describe her as hostile and aggressive. She has developed a deep sense of grievance against the world and has strong resentment against anyone or anything she perceives as 'interfering'.

Susan is now described by various people as 'always looking for trouble', 'trying to pick rows', 'bad tempered' and as having a 'chip on her shoulder'. As her alcohol dependence progresses, Susan has become more stubborn and hard-headed. Quarrels and rows are the order of the day in Susan and Ed's home. Her children are fearful of inviting their friends home in case she is drunk. Even if she isn't drinking there is still the danger that she will be rude to their friends. Her own friends have also started to avoid her because they never know what mood they are going to find her in; whether she will be pleasant or belligerent.

• • •

The 'poor me' attitude

These three women are exhibiting changes in their attitudes, and in their personalities, which reflect their unconscious attempts to ward off any threats to their relationship with alcohol. The changes also reflect their lack of confidence, their discouragement, fear and feelings of inadequacy. Increasingly they are 'self-pitying people'.

Among the outstanding characteristics of the alcohol dependent is the 'poor me' attitude. The entire range of depressed feelings, from sadness to gloom, to misery, to desolation are part of her repertoire. Tied up with this 'poor me' syndrome is the self-centredness of their lives. Increasingly, Susan, Pat and Linda have become obsessed and preoccupied with their alcohol. As the illness progresses, they also set themselves up as the centre of the universe. Other people's needs and feelings become secondary to meeting their own need for alcohol and medicating or relieving their own feelings.

The force of delusion

For family members and friends the most confusing aspect of alcoholism is the woman's denial of the existence of her problem with alcohol. Denial, despite the seemingly obvious and concrete evidence to the contrary.

An understanding of the nature of the condition of

alcohol dependency, or addiction, helps concerned individuals to realise that delusion is a characteristic symptom of alcohol dependency. Delusion is a condition of the mind where someone persistently maintains as true, something which is untrue, or *vice versa*. As one woman described it, 'You believe in your own lies.' When a woman becomes alcohol dependent she also becomes sincerely deluded about her relationship with alcohol. This delusion is *real*, not imaginary. Her mind, imagination and emotional range becomes distorted and concentrated on concealing from herself the true nature of her alcohol dependency. This is a safety valve which protects her from the crippling and overwhelming conflict between her need or perceived need for alcohol and the reality of the consequences of this dependency for herself and others.

An alcoholic woman's perception of her life and her relationships are so badly distorted they cannot give a reliable picture of the true reality. She may continue to affirm that 'everything is fine'. She may deny totally the existence of a problem with alcohol. Instead of recognising the effects of alcohol abuse on her physically, or the effects on her family, she will describe the loving relationship she has with her husband and how well her children are doing. There may be some rationalisation about existing problems that she is admitting to. She may explain that something other than her drinking is the cause of these problems. So, Susan sees Ed's job as the reason for their lack of money, or his tiredness as the reason for their deteriorating sexual relationship. Pat believes that her lack of children caused the breakdown in her marriage. Linda feels that her workmates are envious of her and just getting at her.

A strong defence system

She may deny the truth of some occurrence which others remember because of damage to her memory through blackouts. Most obviously, there is sincere conviction on her part that her denial is valid. This denial is the first line

A Bottle in the Cupboard

of defence. The defence system is a natural psychological system. When someone is bereaved or has experienced a traumatic incident, the defence system is frequently displayed. They may deny that the person is dead, or that the episode occurred. There may be repression of memory. Later they may minimise the consequences by saying 'It wasn't that bad' or 'It was only ...' They may rationalise the situation away by explaining 'Well, it's for the best because ...' or 'It had to happen'. They may also get angry and blame others such as the doctor who was treating the deceased friend, for example.

The defence system of an alcohol dependent woman works in a similar fashion. To others she will minimise the significance of her relationship with alcohol by cutting down to the smallest degree possible the amount she drinks and how frequently she drinks. She will say things like 'I only had one or two' or 'I drink once in a while' or 'It wasn't that bad'. She will also minimise the consequences of her behaviour for other people. So, for example, Susan says that her children aren't affected because she always keeps the house tidy and gives them their dinner every day.

To make excuses and to give alibis and reasons in response to any 'why' questions is second nature for an alcoholic. These reasons give the impression that she is in control of her behaviour, that she did things because she intended to. Thus, when Linda is asked by her mother why she had not come home until 3 am and why she was so drunk, Linda lies. She makes up a tale about missed taxis, great fun and forgetting to call home. It is never the fault of the alcoholic woman, according to the alcoholic. Her fund of reasons, justifications, excuses and people to blame is limitless.

Another defence is to analyse and theorise and speculate. This is a favourite strategy of Susan's. She will spend endless time exploring and discussing why things have happened and how they happened, rather than what actually happened. She works hard at distracting people from her behaviour. She also blames others all the time. 'You made me do it.'

When all else fails, Susan complies. Sometimes she complies angrily. 'Okay, okay, I give in! I'll do it,' when Ed asks her to stop drinking. At other times she is submissive and placatory in her compliance. 'You're right. If you want me to, I'll stop drinking.' This is when she feels Ed is at the end of his tether and she fears he will leave her. However, when Ed takes the pressure off, Susan's compliance ends.

Pat's main defence at this stage of her drinking is repression. She has shut out of her mind anything she doesn't want to look at.

If you were to spend any length of time in Susan's company you would become acquainted with a whole range of defences she has to keep other people at bay. She has developed the practice of ridiculing and belittling people, in particular her children and sometimes their friends. She embarrasses Ed by running him down in company and by being biting in her talk about her neighbours. She is constantly engaged in an ongoing battle with one or other of her neighbours. Sometimes sadness will emerge as a defence, when she will manipulate others to pity her, to give her sympathy, or to protect her. This is the defence she employs most with her sister Joan. She has implied to Joan that Ed is a bad husband, mean with money, violent and aggressive in private and very demanding of her sexually. Joan is bewildered and confused by this. She feels sorry for Susan, knows there is something wrong but feels estranged from Ed because she now believes *he* might be the problem.

Linda also has defensive behaviour. She has become increasingly helpless and inadequate. She will lapse into silence or appear confused when spoken to. Sometimes she talks a lot but she never quite comes to the point, often rambling on or becoming incoherent. All these ploys 'buy her time'.

Other defensive behaviour used by alcoholic women include silence, evasion, sullenness, threats of violence, shouting, arguing, all forms of angry words and gestures and also just ignoring people.

Alcoholic women become mistresses of disguise.

Chapter Seven
The effects of alcohol on family

SUSAN

At times Ed wants to stop living. He has no energy. He has lost contact with his friends. He worries all the time. From the moment he leaves the house in the morning until he discovers in the evening how Susan is, he is anxious, preoccupied and distracted. His work has been affected badly because of the deterioration in his memory and concentration. He finds it difficult to focus on the business in hand. He is edgy, irritable and lacking in creativity.

Ed phones Susan several times a day, checking where she is, waiting for the slurring of her speech which indicates that she has been drinking. Driving home from work is a nightmare for him. His thoughts are totally obsessed with the possible scenarios he may face. He worries about the children and how they are coping, wondering whether Susan will be roaring and screaming at them again.

A family in chaos

On one occasion Ed got home to find Susan sprawled unconscious on the floor. The television was on and their youngest daughter Clare was sitting watching cartoons as if Susan was invisible. Thomas was, as usual, out playing with his mates. Anita, the eldest, was in the kitchen preparing a meal for him. This was normality in their home. That evening he sat on the sofa beside Clare and sobbed uncontrollably. He felt such a failure, so helpless in the face of this problem which he could not seem to deal with. He carried Susan upstairs and put her to bed. They all pretended nothing had happened, ate their meal and talked about other matters. He told Anita that he didn't know what he'd do without her.

The guilt of others

Driving home most evenings Ed's frustration at his life, brings him practically to boiling point. With each promise he believes Susan is able to handle the problem, and the regularity of the disappointments leaves him angry and yet feeling so guilty. He feels unloved and unsupported by Susan and believes he has lost his influence on her. To Ed, Susan's drinking is proof that he is a failure, that he is not a good husband, provider, lover. He feels responsible for the disintegration of their family life and the breakdown of his marital relationship.

He has pleaded and reasoned with Susan to stop drinking on the basis of 'If you loved me you would stop drinking'. When she continued to drink, Ed attempted to force her to change. He withdrew from her, stopped talking to her, snubbed her and ignored her. This too brought failure, and with it came further rejection for Ed. He feels frightened and angry. He is not yet indifferent. He still loves Susan. He blames himself for the difficulties they are having. He believes some of the complaints that Susan persistently makes about her life.

Susan's constant reproaches are made to justify her drinking. 'If you were earning enough money we wouldn't have to live in this house'. 'I hate this house. What's the point in cleaning it? It never looks right'. 'I've no friends here; what else am I supposed to do? Of course I drink. You would too if you were cooped up in this house, in this area'. 'I've too much to do. I have to mind the house, mind the kids and keep a job. I have to drink to keep going'.

These constant complaints make Ed feel inadequate. Susan's other area of attack is their sexual relationship. She has managed to convey to Ed that he is lacking in this area, unable to perform as she requires, as other men could in the past. Of course worry, anxiety, tension and Susan's own incapacity due to alcohol have created the sexual difficulties. Ed's desire for her has declined as the drinking has progressed. Despite the fact that this is another of Susan's desperate attempts to justify her drinking, Ed still feels it is *his* fault.

Although the situation is growing steadily worse, still Ed is refusing to believe in his powerlessness over her drinking. He tries to control her drinking by limiting the availability of money to her, restricting the amount of money she can withdraw from the bank in a week. He drinks with her in the hope that she will somehow begin to drink socially. He asks the children to 'mind' her, to not let her drink, to dispose of any drink they find and not to go to the shops for Susan to buy alcohol. He questions the children about their mother's behaviour and drinking habits.

Attempts to control

Ed doesn't realise yet that Susan is not free to choose about drinking. He is acting on the assumption that she can say 'no' to alcohol. His attempts to control her drinking are sapping his time and energy. Both he and the children are focused on Susan's drinking to the point of obsession. The children are trapped in this war between them and the atmosphere at home is tense, hostile and ready to erupt. The children are anxious and nervous about his return from work, worried about his reactions to Susan. They dread his questions and fear the quarrels and rows between himself and Susan.

At times they too blame Ed, thinking that he is the one at fault. They have overheard Susan complain and have regularly heard the refrain 'You're driving me mad. I have to drink to remain sane in this house'. They believe that if Ed was different, maybe Susan would not drink. They also believe that if Ed would leave her alone, they could have peace in the home. Of course they know Susan is aggressive towards them, but somehow they still blame Ed. They feel torn between their two parents. Ed approves of them when they sabotage Susan's drinking. When he finds her drinking, he frequently gets angry at them. 'Why didn't you pour it out?' he shouts.

Ed's attempts to control Susan's drinking are doomed to failure. The conflict in the house is increasing and she is becoming more defiant and hostile to every suggestion that she cut down on her drinking. Susan feels that everyone is against her, that she has no freedom and no support. She works even harder at hiding her drinking.

A conspiracy of secrecy

Meanwhile, Ed works hard at hiding the problem. Because at some level he feels responsible for the failure of his family to be happy, he is terrified anyone will realise how bad the situation is. He avoids social occasions because he is embarrassed by Susan's behaviour and fearful that friends will learn that she has a problem. He doesn't realise that some of their friends are only too aware of Susan's drinking. However, his embarrassment and tension are so obvious that they balk at mentioning it for fear it will upset him further. They too pretend nothing is happening. They look the other way and seem not to notice when she repeats the same story for the fourth time with the same enthusiasm and interest, as if she has no recollection of her earlier renditions. They smile and joke when she falls asleep on the sofa or the chair. No one ever mentioned again the time she fell asleep in the bathroom halfway through the meal.

Of course as friends avoid the issue, Ed becomes more isolated, and Susan is yet again denied an opportunity to face her alcoholism. That she is suffering from an illness, that she is as powerless as the victim of any other physical or mental illness, has not yet been acknowledged by her friends or her husband. Alcoholism is not sinful, or shameful. It cannot be controlled by will power, the alcoholic's or her partner's. Susan needs help.

Meanwhile, Ed does not speak to anyone, not even family. He has told the children not to discuss Susan's drinking. 'It's no one's business what goes on in our house.' The facade of normality is established. When people visit, they are to see only what is organised for them, including the smile on everyone's face. Everyone is encouraged to keep the 'family secret'.

The enabler

Ed has become the prime enabler of Susan's alcohol dependency. An enabler is anyone who reacts to the symptoms of alcoholism in a way that shields the alcohol dependent person from experiencing the full impact of the harmful consequences of the disease. Each time an enabler excuses the drinking, hides the drinking or shields the drinker, the alcoholic loses an opportunity to gain an insight into the severity of her problem.

Concerned individuals enable because it seems the 'right think to do'. In caring, close relationships we usually support and protect our friends, to help them overcome their problems. We forgive their mistakes, let them know that 'no one is perfect' and that we don't hold resentment. When a woman is alcoholic, friends and family frequently react as if the drinking is a series of isolated incidents or mistakes rather than the symptoms of a progressive and incurable disease. Although enabling is based on a desire to help, it actually worsens the situation.

Enabling often escalates because family members feel responsible for the alcoholic. Joan, Susan's sister, does not confront Susan's drinking because she feels so sorry for her. Susan looks so pathetic when she has been drinking! Joan thinks that if Susan could see herself she wouldn't drink at all. Joan is Susan's older sister and feels protective towards her. She is used to feeling responsible for her. Her first thought on meeting Susan, or phoning her, is 'has she drink on her?' However, Joan has never told Susan this. Joan covers up for Susan with their family; she doesn't want them to know about Susan's drink problem though she knows they can see it for themselves. She feels embarrassed for Susan and acts as if the problem will disappear of its own accord. It is easier for her not to talk about Susan than to admit that she has a problem. Joan does not see Susan as an alcoholic but rather as someone who is using alcohol to cope with pressure. She believes Susan has just 'let things get out of hand'. She too is worried and preoccupied with Susan and frequently has sleepless nights.

Since their parents died, Joan has assumed the position of 'head' of the family and she feels responsible for sorting out Susan's problems. She suffers greatly from stress and her husband John is annoyed with her for focusing so much on Susan. He can clearly see how Susan's problems are affecting Joan. 'If she'd stop drinking there wouldn't be a problem,' he insists. But even John has not realised that Susan is alcoholic and cannot stop drinking. He is angry with Susan and Ed for upsetting his life and avoids them when possible.

How to stop enabling

It is difficult for family members to realise that they need to move away from feeling responsible for the alcoholic. They need to face the truth of the individual's illness, to accept that she is out of control, that she has a disease, that she is an alcoholic. They need to put their pride, shame and fear to one side and act responsibly towards the person who is suffering from alcoholism. They need to stop trying to protect the alcoholic (and members of her family), and realise that they cannot help her until they understand how the addiction, the alcohol dependency, is affecting their own thinking and emotions. Education and outside help is required.

Threats, arguments and pretending the problem does

not exist, is not the way to get results. The family needs to decide on a course of action, with professional help, and to be prepared to act on it. Without insight into her alcoholism, the woman who is alcohol dependent remains a victim of her defences and is incapable of recognising her own need for help. Sometimes family members and friends continue to excuse her drinking and related behaviour because it is seen as normal. 'She deserves to let her hair down now and then', 'It was no big deal last night,', 'Lots of people drink a lot before they're married'. Or sometimes they continue to excuse her behaviour because it is seen as the result of other problems and they believe that her drinking will change as soon as the 'real' problem is resolved. At these times both the alcoholic and the concerned family members, or enablers, are engaged in self-deception.

LINDA

Linda's family are concerned and worried about her. They notice the change in her moods and the change in her personality. Recently her mother Mary has begun to suspect her drinking. She often gets the smell of alcohol from Linda and notices that she is constantly sucking breath fresheners or chewing gum. Linda's mother has asked her about her drinking but Linda gets angry and claims that Mary is always on at her and doesn't trust her. On other occasions Mary is very aware that Linda either does not come home or when she does she is very talkative. It is difficult to follow her conversation and on these occasions Linda starts doing small chores around the house, keeping on the move, as if to try and cover the fact that she has been drinking.

The enablers

Mary and Joe, Linda's parents have been avoiding facing the implications of her excessive drinking for quite some time. They keep hoping the problem will resolve itself without the necessity for action. 'Perhaps it's just a phase, maybe due to the pressure of work?' they wonder. They decide to give her just a little more time. They describe her as 'shy and sensitive' and think of her as somewhat 'troubled' at the moment. They choose to focus on her good qualities, saying 'She is such an intelligent and hard working girl,' and keep giving her another chance. Really they still believe she can stop drinking.

Each time Linda gets drunk, Mary feels sorry for her. When Linda is apologetic and embarrassed the next day, she tries to give her some support by telling her not to worry. However, Mary herself continues to worry and also at times she is very angry with Linda for the upset she is causing in the home. When friends say in passing that they met Linda out at a night club in town, Mary thinks to herself 'Oh no! What do they know about her?' Mary worries about Linda, in case she might injure herself, or get into a compromising or dangerous situation, while drinking.

However, because both Mary and Joe's defences are so strong, because they keep rationalising Linda's drinking, other friends who are also worried about Linda fail to talk to them. The message Mary and Joe have given to the world is 'We're okay. Linda is okay'; 'There's no need to worry. The situation is under control'; 'She's fine except for her job'. Linda's friends pick up the message that Mary and Joe are not really interested in hearing about Linda's drinking problems.

Breaking through

Linda's sister, Pauline, is also concerned about Linda's drinking. She is watching her carefully. She mentally notes the nights Linda is at home and feels temporarily reassured. Linda claims she needs some peace and quiet after work, and that she goes for a drink to unwind. Pauline tries to keep their younger brothers and sisters quiet when Linda comes home, stopping them from asking her about their homework and threatening them about their fighting. She hopes that this would lead to Linda drinking less often. It didn't seem to make any difference. Pauline starts to meet Linda after work, hoping that she could get her home early. She talks to Linda about her drinking and extracts promises from her about cutting down. For periods of time Pauline believes that Linda is controlling her drinking.

Pauline believes she is having some influence over Linda's alcohol consumption because they are 'communicating'. She starts threatening Linda in an attempt to frighten her into stopping. She threatens to tell Linda's bosses about the alcohol problem. Linda laughs at her.

Pauline is embarrassed by Linda's behaviour when drinking. They have many mutual friends who drop hints to her about meeting Linda in town. She has seen how Linda becomes flirtatious and loud with men when drinking, and realises that she has gained a bad reputation within their circle of acquaintances. She feels angry and resentful towards her for being such a burden of worry; she feels frustrated with her for not getting her act together. Pauline worries about the tension Linda is bringing to the family and the worry she is to their parents. She feels very guilty about the fact that she often wishes that Linda would leave home or disappear, so that she could stop having to look out for her and get on with her own life.

On the nights when Linda still isn't home, and it's five o'clock in the morning, Pauline sometimes wishes that Linda would kill herself. This thought frightens her and makes her hate herself. There are good qualities in Linda and they have had many great times together. Unfortunately, Pauline can only think of the heartbreak, worry and anger at the moment. Linda regularly accuses Pauline of being afraid that she would 'make a show' of her. Pauline is always worried that Linda will have a tantrum when drinking. As their younger sisters and brothers say, 'Linda is mad in the head' when drinking.

One day a poster caught Pauline's eye. It was for a group called Al-Anon, run by an organisation set up by the families of alcoholics to help other families affected by alcohol dependency. It said in large red print: 'Does someone you live with drink too much?'

Pauline had to answer yes. The shock of the connection she had just made numbed her. She asked herself the question, 'Does this mean Linda is an alcoholic?'

SUSAN

Anita's Diary

Wednesday 8 September

Dear Diary,

Today was another bad day at school. Miss Higgins the maths teacher got mad at me again. She doesn't seem to believe me that I did try to do my homework. I can't get the hang of these problems. Of course part of the problem is that I kept leaving my homework to check on Clare. I worry so much that she'll do something to annoy Mum. She's too young to know what is happening and she hasn't learned to keep clear of Mum when Mum's in a 'mood'. My attention in class keeps wandering too. Miss Higgins stared at me, and I was miles away. Actually I was wondering if Mum was okay, if she was drinking or not.

Sarah got a new tape for her walkman. She wanted to come around to our house after school to let me hear it. I know she thinks I don't like her but I couldn't be sure that Mum would be okay. I couldn't stand it if she said something to Sarah. Anyway she'd never let me go over to

Sarah's. She'd flip her lid if I didn't help her cook the dinner.

She wasn't in really bad form today. Clare helped me to make fairy buns. Thomas, as usual, was out. It's not fair. He never has to do anything. It's always me. Just because he's a boy! It's Anita this and Anita that. Get me this Anita. Get me that Anita. You're the oldest Anita. I depend on you Anita. You're so good at it Anita. I'm sick of having to stay stuck to her side every day from the minute I get home from school. Well, Dad's home now so I guess I'll get to bed. Goodnight.

Thursday 9 September

Dear Diary,

Got a 'C' in geography for my project. Ann Brown is going out with Paul now. I can't believe it. How does she do it? She's not even good looking. Martha is raging. I hope there won't be a full scale huff on. I can't believe it. Mum's not drinking today either.

Why does she think I'm such a kid? After all I'm fourteen now and most of my friends are going out with boys. I'm old enough to look after Clare, old enough to cook the dinner, clean the house but I'm just someone to boss around. She makes me feel like I'm a nobody. She makes me feel like I have to act like a grown up but then she won't treat me like one.

Dad is as bad. He depends on me but he won't take a stand against her. I have to get going to the disco. Everyone else is going. I'll go mad if I have to stay in this house one more evening. She's always interfering. Dad seems to care, but I wonder. Sometimes it feels like I'm an outsider in this house, which I am. I've no one to talk to and no one cares about me.

Friday 10 September

Dear Diary,

I hate her. Why does nothing ever go right for me? Dad came home early. He hardly said hello. He was straight in there, sussing out Mum. I asked him about the disco but he wouldn't answer me. I nearly told him about the bottle in the washing machine. But why should I? Then he'd have really been in his element, cross-examining me, then giving out to her. As it is, he wouldn't speak a word to anyone all evening. Just because she'd had a few. I said 'sorry for living' to him. Dad was making me feel I was in the way.

Wherever I am these days, I feel in the way. I wonder why they ever had kids. Dad's good but he's not like a real father, someone to love. He doesn't show his feelings or anything like that. Neither does she for that matter, only when she's trying to make up to you. Then it's only false feelings. She thinks I believe her when she's being real nice to me but I know. I know it never lasts. You're just waiting for the moment she's going to pounce on you.

I hope everything will work out for me and I won't be too complicated. I don't want to be like her. Please don't let me ever be like her. It won't be through my fault if I am. I'm going to make my life work. All I want is love, happiness, security. Surely that's not too much to ask. I'm not going to make the same mistakes they did. They never really treated me as a daughter. They just treat me as someone who lives here. Maybe I grew up too quick. She never tried to understand me. Surely they both know what the problem is. She must be ridden with guilt, but she'll never stop, will she? Oh no. Promises, promises. Then she just puts me down and tells me I'm useless. She tells me I've no personality, that I'm no good, no help, that no one loves her. No one loves her! She just starts at you for no reason, saying nasty things.

I could go on forever but you've heard it all before, Diary. Like the weekend I nearly did it. I stayed in my room. I was really, really depressed. I think I was

101

beginning to go mad, but they just went about as usual, arguing and bickering. I know she just wanted rid of him so she could get sloshed. Thomas was gone as usual. He was staying the night in Paddy's. Why do I always have to be stuck here? Dad went off to play golf and she started straight away. She was pissed in about half an hour. Then she started 'Anita this, Anita that'. Finally she said she was tired and was going to lie down on the sofa. I knew she'd be out for the count. Dad would be home and he'd be livid. It would be all my fault as usual.

I had twenty tablets that I found in her room. I took four to start with and then two more. I couldn't take any more. I don't know what stopped me. Maybe it was the thought of her crying and lamenting, pretending she cared. Perhaps I couldn't bear the thought of her acting.

Saturday 11 September

Dear Diary,

Had a nice day today. Maybe it was because I got out of the house. Dad took me shopping. For once we got away without her. We went in for our lunch afterwards. She's not drinking today. I can't believe it. We were both on edge coming back to the house. Dad was doing that little whistle he does when he's worrying. But everything was okay. Mum was in good form. We all had a nice tea and watched a video. Goodnight.

Sunday 12 September

Dear Diary,

I knew it was too good to last. I'm up in my room nearly all day. There's no sign of things getting any better. What a life! I've got Clare up here with me. She's driving me mad, but I've no choice. I've got no one really. No one understands. I can't tell my friends, but then I've no real friends, no one to talk to. Clare is too young. She doesn't understand. I need to get away from here. Please, God. God I'm really afraid of her, really I am. She pulled me off my chair in the middle of dinner.

Why have I such a bitch of a mother? Why does she

make it so hard for me? Why is life so hard on me? I don't mind that I don't get on with her but why does she make it so hard for me? Why won't God help me? I'm so fed up and so depressed that words couldn't express how I feel. You're the only one I can tell.

Dad always says he'll sort it out, not to be worrying Gran and Pops, but he doesn't. He just keeps her happy. Then it's all over, all smoothed away as if it never happened. But what about me? I must be just a nothing. No one cares how I feel. I am going mad. I've lost nearly all hope at this stage. What can I do? She keeps laughing at me. Well she's done it this time. She was definitely drunk at church and she must have been at it while she was making the dinner. We must have missed a bottle. I wonder where she had it. She must have got it while we were out shopping yesterday. No wonder she was in such good form. It's always the calm before the storm in this house.

If they really loved us they'd be different. She would at least try. Families are supposed to be about having a mother who loves you and looks after you and a father who teaches and helps you. You do things together. You laugh and have a bit of fun. Why can't our family be like that? Why can't we all go to bed and have a quiet night's sleep without warring and shouting going on? All I want is a little bit of peace.

This family is no good – it's useless. Maybe all families are useless. Maybe growing up means you learn you have to depend on yourself. When I am old enough I don't think I'll have a family. I'll have a career. I've had enough of families. I've had enough of looking after this one. Anyway I might make a mess of a family. I think I'm cold, just like Dad says Mum is.

If I was a man I'd leave my wife if she drank like Mum does. I'd take the kids too. Drink just messes up kids. Mum's always too busy or too drunk to pay any attention to us. She's too wrapped up in herself. Sometimes I like her, but does she like me? I wouldn't mind her drinking every now and then if she didn't get so angry. As it is she ignores me even when she isn't drinking. All I want is to be noticed. She's disgusting. She's not like a mother at all. I still think she could stop if she cared enough. I'm always afraid no one will ever like me or love me. I always feel different. Some people pity me. I'm afraid they'll think I'm like my mother.

The children of alcoholics

Anita's diary is reflective of many of the concerns of children of alcoholic mothers. There is much resentment among children about the consequences of drinking. They frequently express shame of their alcoholic mother and feel rejected by both parents, the non-alcoholic one as well as the alcoholic. They feel more deeply affected by the disharmony and the rejection at home than by the drinking. This does not mean that children are not concerned about their mother's drinking but their main concern is the constant parental unhappiness and quarrelling.

Children seem to feel that a woman in particular shouldn't drink and frequently describe their mother's drinking as 'not like a mother'. This seems to reflect the double standard of society about women drinking which children pick up at an early age. Most children feel that both parents are inconsistent and unpredictable, not just the alcoholic. They worry about the effect on the non-drinking parent. Many children lose respect for both parents. 'How can you respect your parents when they act as they do?' 'I'm too ashamed to let my friends know them' is a recurrent theme.

Children never forget their experiences with violence, destructiveness and abuse. They remember incidents that occurred when they were only toddlers. Frequently parents console themselves that their children are too young to understand, to know what is happening. But even a small baby has the full range of emotional capacity. Perhaps they cannot intellectually understand or verbalise their reactions but they react emotionally and experience the tension, the fear, the anger. They are very vulnerable because in order to cope they internalise the problem and believe it to be their fault.

Children need to feel safe with a parent. When they are afraid or unable to trust their parent or parents they feel very insecure. They prefer to believe that *they* are in the wrong and thus deny that they are being abused; they pretend to have a safe parent. When they are ashamed, their self-image and self-confidence become badly distorted.

Most children worry about financial problems. 'We never have money to do the things other kids do. Mum makes me lie to people when they call to the door. Dad seems to be working all the time, but I think Mum must be drinking it all away'.

These children worry a lot. 'I keep worrying about what will happen'. 'I worry all the time'. 'I'm always confused. Mum and Dad never agree on anything. You can't talk to Mum. She never minds what you say as long as you're on her side. You can't please her. You have to do everything she says. She's always at Dad. All the fighting makes me feel so nervous. They never think of us. It's impossible not to take sides. Sometimes you're on one side and then on the other.'

The children of alcoholic parents need treatment. As it says in the Children's Bill of Rights:

> For every child, understanding and guiding her/his personality as her/his most precious gift. For every child, a home and that love and security which a home provides — an environment harmonious and enriching, free from conditions which tend to thwart her/his development.
>
> For every child a community which recognises and plans for her/his needs and protects her/him against physical danger, moral hazard and disease.
>
> For every child such teaching and training as will prepare her/him for successful parenthood and, for parents, supplementary training to fit them to deal wisely with the problems of parenthood.

Chapter Eight
Breaking the pattern

SUSAN

Ed felt like a new man. It was as if the weight of the world had been lifted off his shoulders. Sunday was the last straw. He had reached the point where he could no longer pretend that he could cope. Susan had been drunk in church, drank more when she returned home, hit and pulled at Anita during Sunday lunch, screamed and shouted at him and then passed out in the living room. He stood there looking at her; the children had disappeared up the stairs, white-faced and crying. His wife had an alcohol problem. The evidence was there in front of his eyes. Matters were not improving.

Light and hope
On Monday morning he phoned a number he had kept in his wallet from an advertisement he had read weeks (or was it months?) previously: a counsellor, specialising in addiction problems. On Tuesday evening, putting to one side his worries about what was happening at home, Ed attended his first appointment. In one hour he talked so much he amazed himself. All the worries, concerns and fears of the last years just poured out in a flood of words. Finally he had admitted to someone else 'My wife drinks too much.'

Why had it been so hard to put into words what he had thought so often? Like many other men, Ed found it difficult to admit even to himself that his wife is an alcoholic. Like many other men, through fear and pride, he didn't let anyone know he needed help. Like many other men Ed was overcome with shame. 'What will people think? What will I say?' Ed believed that he, in his perceived role as head of the family, should have been able to see to it that Susan stopped drinking.

Now, after one session, he has a greater understanding that Susan is not able to 'give up alcohol' by a simple exercise of will power. He is starting to understand that she is actually suffering from a disease, that she cannot see clearly what is happening to her and to the family.

Ed has been advised not to threaten, bribe or punish Susan in an attempt to get her to stop drinking. He has also been advised not to dump alcohol or hide bottles; not to drink with her; not to cover up the problems caused by her drinking; not to take over her responsibilities and not to demand or accept unrealistic promises about not drinking. In other words, he has been advised not to try to control Susan's drinking, but to leave her free to drink without restriction.

This scares Ed greatly, because he still wants to protect them all from the consequences of Susan's drinking. He has gained a glimmer of awareness about how preoccupied he has become with Susan's drinking, but it is still difficult to take in. To help him understand these new perspectives Ed has also been advised to go to Al-Anon. It has been explained to him that he will gain support there for himself. Al-Anon is a fellowship of help for the family and friends of alcoholics. The notion that other people have the same worries and fears as Ed, had never really occurred to him. That there was somewhere to go, somewhere that could offer him answers to questions like 'How did this happen? Am I to blame? What did I do wrong? What can I do to help? Does anybody else feel like I do? How can I feel better?' offers Ed hope.

Hope. At long last. He has realised finally that he cannot treat Susan's alcoholism himself. He desperately wants Susan to recover. He wants to believe that normality can be restored to his marriage and to his family and that there can be a better life in the future. Today he was told that it is possible. He doesn't quite believe it, not yet.

Several weeks later Ed is beginning to believe that things could change. He certainly wants something better for himself. In Al-Anon he has learned that he must change his own attitude, that he must let go of being over-protective of, and over-responsible for, Susan's drinking. He has found it difficult, but he is no longer making excuses for her. He is no longer letting her drinking interfere with his plans. He has realised that Susan's life revolved more and more around alcohol, so his life revolved more and more around Susan. His job, his hobbies and in particular the children all lost out. Finally Ed has accepted that Susan has a problem that he cannot solve and that it is not cowardly to give up, to let go.

Intervention

Through his sessions with the addiction counsellor Ed has come to the realisation that he must intervene in Susan's drinking. He has more energy now because he is no longer totally preoccupied with her. He feels supported by his counsellor and his new friends in Al-Anon. Importantly, he has spoken to his own brother and also Susan's sister, Joan, about his concerns. He has learned how to communicate with Susan about her drinking. He is starting to give her feedback, describing her drinking and how it affects him. He now knows to do this in a concerned way, without criticising and only when Susan is not drinking. He tries to tell her when he is upset or disappointed or worried, despite the discomfort they both feel. He has learned to give specific details about what has happened on particular occasions. He talks to her about her irresponsible behaviour and backs it up with details of his worry, concern and fears for her.

By keeping this level of awareness uppermost in their relationship, Ed has reached the stage where he hopes to help Susan accept her alcoholism. He has made a decision with the support of his counsellor and Al-Anon. He intends to confront Susan with the help of Joan and his brother. Using the guidelines provided by the addiction counsellor, Ed intends to request that Susan seeks guidance by going for an assessment interview in a treatment centre for alcohol and drug dependency. He expects that Susan will be defensive and hostile, that she will be threatened by any suggestion that she stop drinking. However, in a concerned manner, they intend to present Susan with the evidence of the problems caused by her drinking, her failures to stop drinking and their worry for her health and peace of mind.

They will ask her to seek professional guidance about the severity of her problem. They know they will need to be strong and certain about their request for this, that Susan will have many excuses and justifications to cover her refusal. However, they intend to be adamant in their request — that Susan attend an assessment interview at a treatment centre for alcohol and drug dependency.

LINDA

Meanwhile, Pauline, through her attendance at Al-Anon, has reached a similar stage in her awareness of her sister Linda's alcoholism. Linda's drinking has been causing major problems at work. She has let it slip, while drinking, that she has been cautioned by the personnel officer. Pauline has decided to take a strong stand. She has contacted Linda's personnel officer and arranged a meeting with her, to share her worries about Linda's drinking. Pauline knows she is taking a large risk, that Linda will be extremely angry, resentful and bitter about

Pauline's interference in her life. Pauline, however, with Al-Anon's help, has come to understand the seriousness of Linda's 'drinking problem'. She now accepts that Linda is alcoholic, that it is a progressive illness which will not disappear but which will get worse. She now realises that Linda is protective of her drinking and cannot see the deterioration in herself. She knows Linda loves her job but that she is in very real danger of losing it.

Pauline recognises that the crisis in Linda's career is an ideal opportunity to use some leverage to further Linda's awareness of the need to seek help. Pauline knows that Linda is anxious about her job. She also knows that if possible she will try to gain a reprieve by fervent promises to placate her employers. Pauline has had no success in her attempts to get a commitment from Linda to seek help. She wants to bring this crisis with Linda's employer out in the open. By negotiating with Linda's personnel officer she hopes that the next crisis created by Linda in her job through her drinking will be the one which will put pressure on her to do something about her drinking.

SUSAN

Susan's assessment has gone well. She has listened to the assessment officer's diagnosis of alcoholism and the description of the implications of dependency. She has been made aware of the availability of help and the different services available. She has remained defensive, even hostile. She has been encouraged to accept further help, and to explore the avenues open to her. She has protested right through the interview that she can stop drinking, any time, but it is obvious that she is listening carefully.

Susan displayed little reaction other than anger when initially confronted by Ed and Joan. Her understanding of the distress experienced by her family is limited. Surprisingly, however, she did agree to go for the assessment. Now, when faced with a clear diagnosis of alcoholism, Susan looks pale and shocked. When she asks a direct question about the cost of treatment and its format, Ed is startled. He reassures her that this is covered by their medical insurance. When Susan agrees to enter an in-patient treatment programme, Ed is stunned.

LINDA

Linda meanwhile has agreed to go for out-patient treatment for her alcoholism and to attend A.A. She had goofed up again at work, she had reached the limits of her sick leave and her job was on the line. It had been made quite clear that her sick leave record, her punctuality and the quality of her work were such that unless she agreed to do something about her drinking they would have no alternative but to terminate her contract.

● ● ●

Treatment

For many women, entering a treatment centre is something which they will fight against. Like many alcohol dependents, male and female, they may not consider themselves to be alcoholics. They may fear the stigma of such a label or they may be so deluded and so defensive that they have no understanding or acceptance of the nature of their condition. They may not see the connection between the problems in their life, the feedback they have received about their behaviour and attitudes, and their drinking. They may be detached emotionally from the distress experienced by their family and friends. They may

111

be terrified by the prospect of life without alcohol. They may be angry and full of blame about the difficulties they are experiencing.

Women are particularly reluctant to go for treatment. Often women are already economically dependent and so the awareness of irresponsibility and unmanageability are centred on their roles as wives and mothers. Because these roles are so central to many women's self-image, they are usually more rigidly defensive than men about the effects of their drinking on family.

For alcoholic men, cultural attitudes and bar-room myths perpetuate the comforting notion that men do not have to be involved parents, that if they contribute financially to their children's rearing this is sufficient. For this reason, men can convincingly believe that their drinking is not affecting their children.

Because a woman who is a mother is seen as filling the role of the carer, a role that demands committed practical support to her children and also emotional support, it is more difficult for a woman to rationalise and justify the limitations in her relationship with her children because of her drinking. The shame is deeper, as is the guilt. Her need to defend, to deny, is all the greater. For women the acceptance of their alcoholism seems to be extremely difficult as is the admission of their disease to others. Women's excessive drinking is culturally less acceptable than men's and this is reflected in the attitude of those around the woman, including her children. It is also reflected in her own attitude, her own lack of self-respect, self-esteem or self-worth. At the heart of it, she too believes it is worse that she, a woman, should be an alcoholic.

Few dependent people enter treatment with a clear view of their alcoholism. Most will deny the problem. Through the process of education and identification with other ¯addicts they gain a new understanding of the severity of their problem and the extent of the consequences to themselves and to their family and friends. This is usually a gradual process. Many treatment programmes have a combination of several elements: lectures, discussions, talks by recovering addicts, group therapy and individual therapy. For those in in-patient programmes there is also the element of community living and attendance at the appropriate fellowships of Alcoholics Anonymous and/or Narcotics Anonymous. Most treatment programmes encourage family participation. Alcohol dependency is seen as a condition which also affects family members.

Acceptance of the illness

One of the main goals of treatment is to accept that alcoholism is one of the unchangeable aspects of the sufferer's life, that she is powerless over this, and that as a result of alcoholism her life has become unmanageable. To do this, she needs to understand the chronic and incurable nature of alcoholism. She also needs to explore how her relationship with alcohol has affected her life, the choices she has made, the decisions she has made, how she has spent her time, energy and money in the pursuit of meeting her need to drink. She is encouraged to explore this by talking and writing about her drinking history and the events in her life throughout this period. She is helped to become aware of her attitudes, defences and behaviour through feedback from group members, counsellors and family members. She is encouraged and supported to listen to others.

Family members are encouraged to help her by reflecting back to her *their* feelings and thoughts about specific incidents and occasions when she was drinking. In this way, others hold their own personal mirror up for the alcoholic that she might view herself through their eyes. This may be frightening, distressing and uncomfortable for her but with the support of group members and counsellors she can come to see herself as she really is, rather than in a deluded, defensive way.

She needs to be offered this opportunity to gain insight into how her alcohol dependency affects her and others.

For perhaps the first time in years she is helped to see clearly the consequences of her choice to drink. No longer will she be able to claim 'I didn't know' or 'I didn't mean it'. One of the aims of treatment is to bring her to a crossroad in her life, without the fog of delusion and denial, where she can decide which direction she wishes to travel. She can then choose either the road to alcohol dependency, with the knowledge of the consequences that it has brought and will bring, or the road to sobriety.

Visualising the future

The alcoholic woman needs then to be helped to visualise what the future could offer her if she became sober. For most, if not all, alcoholics the view of the future without alcohol is a grey, bleak one. They need to be helped to re-establish goals for the future and to develop rewarding relationships with those important others in their lives: husband, boyfriend, children, lover, parents, brothers and sisters, friends. Focus also will be moved to the development of positive self-esteem and survival skills.

The dependent person is supported to make changes in her behaviour which will create and cultivate positive experiences. With a confidential group of people with similar experiences and similar problems where there is a mutual contact of shared support, honesty and disclosure of feelings and thoughts, tremendous relief is experienced by the alcoholic woman. She learns that she can help others and be important to them. The admission of common experiences and feelings give her the realisation that she is not unique or alone. The disquieting and uncomfortable fears that she is 'mad' or 'bad' or 'different', which have been heightened by her defensiveness and social isolation, are expelled by the growing awareness that others think, feel, lack feeling and behave in a similar fashion.

The shared honesty of mutual weaknesses gives her the courage to face up to her own problems and difficulties. Within a safe and supportive environment she has the opportunity to express her feelings and talk openly about issues in her life.

Many people who become alcoholic have major problem areas in their lives. Some of the issues may pre-date the drinking; some may result from alcohol dependency. Many addicts may have been physically or sexually abused as children. They often see themselves as the 'victim' in life and are reluctant or find it difficult to see beyond that role. They may lack trust in people and be fearful of involving themselves in any close or intimate relationship. They may have grown up with alcoholic or emotionally rejecting parents. They may be badly scarred emotionally by traumatic events in their lives and have used alcohol as a crutch or cushion to protect themselves or to deny very real emotional pain.

Some women retreat into alcohol and/or drug dependency as an attempt to cope with or survive their life experiences: failed marriages, abusive or alcoholic husbands, rejection, desertion. Many older women resort to alcohol when their families have grown up and left home. They may be left in a loveless marriage or alone without a companion, having lost their main function, purpose and motivation in life. They fill the hole in their existence with alcohol, passing their days in a hazy stupor.

Sexuality and fertility

Other issues which women in treatment for alcohol dependency often face are issues around sexuality and fertility. Many have had miscarriages, abortions or have been unable to conceive much longed-for children. They may have sexual difficulties and problematic sexual relationships. Studies have documented the association between alcoholism among women and their experiences of both physical and sexual abuse. Comparing alcoholic women and non-alcoholic women, much higher percentages of alcoholic women have been victims of domestic violence, violent crime, rape and assault. Other studies have shown high rates of victimisation by individuals other than family members, spouses or lovers.

The image of the alcoholic woman as an acceptable target of sexual aggression was illustrated by the widely publicised rape case in Bedford, Massachusetts (1983) when an intoxicated twenty-two-year-old woman was raped by six men on a pool table in a bar, while others present ignored her calls for help, or urged the rapists on. During the trial, townspeople picketed the courthouse, protesting that the victim got what she asked for, with the implied attitude that any woman who exposes herself drunk to men should expect no better.

This case revealed a frightening attitude toward women who drink. The 'fallen woman' stereotype of the female alcoholic is still alive and well, no change since fourteenth-century Chaucer in the *Canterbury Tales* expressed the attitude that 'A woman in her cups has no defence.' There is a culturally ignored expectation of sexual promiscuity that leads to the stigmatisation of alcoholic women. This persists despite an absence of supporting data. 'Indeed the idea that an alcoholic woman is an immoral "fallen" woman may increase her acceptability as a target for abuse of all kind,' suggests Sheila Blume MD, in her article exploring this issue.

She also points out that prolonged heavy drinking is a major cause of sexual and reproductive dysfunction in women. In fact, alcohol intake has been found to suppress physiological sexual arousal in women. Increasing blood alcohol levels lead to decreased intensity of orgasm, and lessens desire. However, 60 per cent of non-abstaining women reported that they sometimes or usually felt less inhibited about sex when drinking. In an 1986 study (Klassen and Wilsnack) only 8 per cent of drinking women reported positively when asked whether they became 'less particular' in their choice of sexual partner when drinking. Sixty per cent of the women reported that 'someone else who had been drinking became sexually aggressive' towards them.

The shame and guilt which an alcoholic woman carries

for this perception that she is 'fair game' or 'looking for it' is a recurring issue within treatment. The prejudices of society in general and that of her family, friends and neighbours in particular, often make group therapy a difficult process for a woman in treatment. She is frequently faced with her male fellow-alcoholics' judgements about her drinking. Again she may have to deal with being perceived as an acceptable target for abuse.

Personal power and control

The whole issue of personal power and control is a central one for the alcoholic woman. Many are very manipulative and adept at exerting influence in a subtle way over others. They may have grown up in a situation where they had little personal power or freedom of choice; in a home with a dominant, aggressive father or abusive parent, either physically, sexually or verbally. Though often presenting an outward image of helplessness and weakness, many alcoholic women become expert at getting their own way either by flattery, compliance or by an appeal for sympathy and pity. Often they use their alcoholism as an expression of anger and frustration about their life.

Initially to drink may have been the only form of perceived 'freedom' open to them. They have rebelled and stood up for themselves by drinking. Within the safety of the group, in therapy, they can begin to express their feelings of shame, guilt, fear and anger. They can begin to recognise how alcoholism stole their freedom rather than liberated them and can explore the options open to them to meet their own needs in a constructive healthy manner. They are given permission to own their feelings of helplessness, hurt, loss and grief and to build new avenues of growth and investment in life.

There is no deed or thought which is fully beyond the experience of others. As other group members express their identification with her feelings and behaviour and their understanding of her problems, it becomes easier for the alcoholic to forgive herself, to understand herself, to accept herself. As she shares her deepest concerns, fears and secrets it becomes easier for her to believe that she is acceptable, warts and all.

Saying 'no' to alcohol

For the alcoholic woman the growth of awareness and insight about the nature and extent of her illness, allows her to develop more rewarding and honest relationships, and so she gains understanding of herself, her life and the problems she faces; thus she becomes ready to accept responsibility for her own individual growth. Now she realises that *she* chose her alcohol, and that *she* returned to it again and again, because she loved it and what it did for her, rather than explore other options and possibilities. With this awareness comes the responsibility to say 'no' to alcohol, to opt for all those other choices she is learning in treatment.

SUSAN

On entry into treatment, Susan felt confused and angry. She was angry with Ed and Joan for pushing her into this, frightened about the future and unsure of what she thought or felt about anything. She didn't know where to start. She was full of pain, self-loathing and despair. She had felt desperation for quite a while. Every drink she took nearly choked her; she hadn't enjoyed her alcohol for nearly a year. Everyday she asked herself 'What am I doing?' Everyday she believed more and more that she was a bad person, a weak person. Why couldn't she stop? She felt like there was a 'hungry monster deep inside me. He kept roaring for drink! drink! drink! all day long. I spent my days trying to fill him and he was never satisfied.' Some days she looked at herself in the mirror trying to see this monster deep inside.

Now she is learning that will-power cannot stop an alcoholic drinking, and that this is because they are out of control; to hear other people identifying with this; to hear this feeling described as 'powerlessness'; to begin to believe that she is not going mad; that maybe there is hope for her after all. This is all such a relief for Susan that, after her first day in treatment she sat in her bedroom and cried. The counsellors seemed so unsurprised, so matter-of-fact about it all. They seemed to recognise everything they were being told as predictable and expected in alcohol dependency. Maybe after all God hadn't forgotten her.

Susan still has fears. She fears that she is a hopeless case, that she may not be able to change. She fears life without alcohol. She fears her own feelings and problems and thinks she may not be able to cope. However, already she is contemplating the possibility of change and life without alcohol. Listening to other alcoholic women and men in A.A., in the treatment centre, talking about their drinking, treatment and recovery gave her some hope that things could be different.

As the days and weeks moved on Susan began to realise with shock how affected Ed and the children had been. She had always blamed Ed, she had never really believed he loved her and recently he had become so critical and cold towards her she had been convinced he didn't care at all. To hear him talk about his constant worry and concern, his loneliness and isolation, the times he cried himself to sleep, was a revelation to her.

When she read a letter from Anita talking about the way Susan had behaved towards her, the times she was drunk and incapable of even sitting on a chair and how the children were frightened and angry with her, she wept bitterly. She began to see herself as they did; the angry, resentful, bitter, aggressive drunk, Susan, and she didn't like it.

She could see at the same time how they were all trying to be nice to her. They visited her, talked to her about what was happening at home, told her how much they loved her and wanted her back. It didn't fit! She was such a nasty person, how could they still want her? Even the day when Ed got angry and spoke of how she neglected the children, he still said he wanted her to get well, to be a well, loving person again, rather than someone he had to mind and protect the children from.

Susan began to learn about how alcohol dependency is an emotional disease and how it affects the entire family. She learnt how family members' feelings become buried and suppressed, how they enabled her in their attempts to cope with the situation. She remembered that Clare constantly questioned her about what she had in her mug, even checking on her by having a sip from the mug sometimes. She realised now, with horror, that even Clare had known better than herself that there was a problem with alcohol. She had been so shut off, so self-protective; she had thought of no one but herself. Ed had been trying so hard to stop her, to protect the family. Anita had been trying to keep her happy, to become the 'little mother' of the home, over-responsible and too old for her years. Thomas had fled from the home, seeking peace away from her. Susan feels so much remorse and guilt, but the group has helped her to see that as positive if she uses it to help herself make certain the future is different by not drinking.

One day her counsellor said something which made everything fall into place. She said 'Susan, if you can think of the person you want to be, the sort of woman, wife, mother, friend you believe in and the way you'd like to live your life, then you can see who you really are. That is the real Susan, with all the values and standards she possesses. All you need to do is remove the obstacles that stop you being the person you really are. Everything else has been a mistake.'

There and then Susan finally realised it. A huge weight seemed to be lifted off her shoulders. Without alcohol she could live as she believed she ought to live, as she wanted to live. Her husband, children, family and friends still loved her. They had lost her to alcohol, for a time, but Susan was still here after all. She began to cry. She felt so peaceful, so grateful.

• • •

It is two years later. Susan and Linda have become firm friends despite the difference in their age and in their life situation. They met at A.A. on Susan's first day out of her in-patient treatment programme. Linda was still attending her out-patient programme. They chatted and realised that they had one special date in common; they had both taken their last drink on the same day. They have taken a vow to keep it their last. They have celebrated two 'birthdays' now and intend to make it sixty-two, if they live that long.

• • •

Pat, who lived alone, was found dead in bed. The death certificate said heart failure but the bedroom was strewn with empty bottles. Pat was one of the unlucky women alcoholics, a woman who did not get a second chance at life.

• • •

The road to recovery is not a smooth or easy one. Chapter Nine charts the recovery process and its effect on the alcoholic, her family and friends.

Chapter nine
The road to recovery

Recovery

At last you, or the alcoholic in your life, has admitted alcohol dependency. You have reached the point where you feel you cannot go on any more as you are. You are finally willing to get help. Don't let this chance slip by. Don't let others talk you out of this admission even if they say, 'Oh, you're not a bad person. You couldn't be an alcoholic?' or 'I didn't know you drank that much. Are you sure you're an alcoholic?'

Perhaps you are still saying, 'I'll quit tomorrow.' Maybe you are saying to yourself, 'I'm stopping drinking now,' and think you can do it on your own without telling anyone or admitting to anyone, other than yourself, that you are an alcoholic. Maybe you have stopped drinking, for a while. Whatever stage of the recovery you have reached, the first and most important thing to realise about recovery is that you cannot do it on your own. It's not a coincidence that the first word of the first step of the Twelve Step Programme of Alcoholics Anonymous is 'We'. Very few alcoholics manage to give up alcohol without some kind of support system.

Professional help

It is important to seek some kind of professional guidance at the early stages of recovery. A professional assessment officer can help you become aware of the extent of your problem and also guide you in your decision regarding the kind of support you need during recovery. They will help you to recognise whether you require specialised professional support in the form of residential treatment or outpatient treatment. You may be convinced that you can stop drinking without outside help, and may be determined to try. Perhaps the financial commitment involved in agreeing to treatment worries you, or the commitment of time and energy makes you uneasy. You may have children and find residential treatment difficult to arrange. Even if money and childminders are available you may have intense guilt and resistance to leaving your children for a period of time. Such guilt and unease will be real even if, rationally, you know that the children will not be safe until you make sure of your sobriety. Another cause of resistance to treatment is embarrassment, plain and simple. How do you explain where you are going for a period of several weeks? What if you meet someone you know? Who will see you entering the clinic every day? Because of the social stigma attached to being an alcoholic woman, you will probably be highly sensitive to this aspect of resistance to treatment.

Very often a woman will delay coming for treatment, denying her problem until no other course is open to her. Her family will also cover up for her. By the time she appears for treatment her self-respect is likely to be practically nil. Because the disease process is telescoped, ie gets worse faster, for an alcoholic woman, she will be further into chronic alcoholism than her male equivalent. Emotionally she will be more rigidly defensive and detached from the conflict her drinking is creating for her. She may be so guilt-ridden that she is unable to see an acceptable way out or believe or hope that she can change. She is more likely than her male counterpart (the male alcoholic) to believe that she is a bad and wicked person, an unnatural person, or a mad person. Women reach higher blood alcohol concentrations than men when drinking an equal quantity of alcohol. Consequently they have a more marked history of intoxication and acting-out, which in turn adds to their developing sense of low self-esteem.

The role of counsellor/therapist

For all the reasons mentioned earlier in this book the woman alcoholic is likely to be physically in worse shape than her male counterpart and this will be exacerbated if she delays treatment. Remember, if you suffer from this illness, the role of a counsellor or therapist is to serve as a guide; to help you gain knowledge of your illness and its effects on your body; to help you become aware of your attitudes, your thinking; to help you learn how alcohol curtails, suppresses and distorts your emotions and feelings.

The goal for treatment is to help you become more comfortable and at ease in the world, able to handle your life without alcohol. The counsellor is also there to support and encourage. She or he cannot do the trip for you, but can certainly point the way. Treatment is not about making you stop drinking but rather about creating an atmosphere in which you are better able to choose sobriety for yourself. It will bring you to a point where you can see the crossroads more clearly without the fog or haze of alcohol clouding and distorting the options. Treatment can help you appreciate where drinking is bringing you and what it has done already to you and your family. Treatment provides an opportunity to explore the possibility of recovery and to take those first few frightening steps towards honesty and responsibility, towards a different relationship with yourself, your partner, your children or your family and friends.

Treatment is a safe, supportive place where you can take risks with the help of your counsellors and fellow addicts. It may still feel frightening and threatening, as does anything new, but you will not be alone in it. Recovery is a journey. It is not an isolated event. It is not about just stopping drinking. How far you want to travel, where your destination will be in terms of the changes made, depends on you. How you travel is your choice also; who you choose to support you, what you do every day to work on your recovery, whether you use a treatment programme or a therapist, or the fellowship of Alcoholics Anonymous.

Where to begin?

The first step in any journey is to know where to start. Unless you can see clearly where your feet are, you are likely to miss your step. Treatment can help you start to see what your life is really about and where you are, indeed who you are. But it is still only a first step. The journey continues after treatment. It is a lifelong process, a one-day-at-a-time process. Each day you begin recovery afresh; each day you will need to find time to work for your recovery, to value yourself and the freedom sobriety brings.

Every woman's recovery is individual to her; it is her personal journey to self-knowledge, self-awareness, self-esteem, self-confidence and self-worth. Recovery is not about abstinence only, or non-indulgence or alcohol deprivation. It is not about living with fear and anxiety. Rather it is about learning the joy of living. The healing process around recovery takes time. The sufferer will have been very hurt and damaged by her alcoholism, and if she appears to be coping well, this is because she is more expert than most at hiding her feelings and fears.

Trusting for recovery

Alcohol has been so important in the alcoholic's life that when she stops drinking there is a great gap in her life. Something has to take its place.

If you can, imagine life represented by a tray which contains many different compartments of varying sizes and shapes. These compartments represent different aspects of life, parents, children, partner, job, hobbies, friends. Only one of those compartments is for alcohol.

People fill these segments to varying degrees. Some have more in the segment representing family. Some have more in the segment representing work. The alcoholic woman starts filling the segment representing alcohol but when it is full she continues to pour. She pours more and more alcohol into her life and it continues to overflow into the other compartments, washing out what they contained. Very soon the tray of life is afloat with alcohol, perhaps even saturated with it. Depending on when she stops drinking, there will be several compartments washed out or awash with alcohol. When alcohol is gone those sections will be distressingly empty. This is to be expected. Alcoholics who try to carry on, without putting anything in the place of drugs or alcohol, eventually fail.

When the alcoholic woman stops drinking, when she has overcome the physical withdrawals, then she is faced with the emptiness, the black hole inside, the feeling of 'What's the point anyway?' She may know alcohol has caused problems but that doesn't necessarily mean it has lost its attraction. After all it is familiar. Recovery may not mean much at this point. She may tell herself, or others may be telling her, that it will be great, that it will bring happiness beyond her wildest dreams; but this may mean nothing. She cannot imagine it, she cannot feel it. This is why recovery is very often an act of faith, a walking over the cliff, a leap in the dark. She may not know where she is going, where she will end up or how she will feel about it. This is very frightening and risky, no matter how determined she is to recover. Even if she is very sure that she does not want the life she has led while drinking, recovery takes courage.

It is normal that she will be feeling vulnerable, anxious and afraid. It is normal that she will experience a grieving for her alcohol, a sense of loss that may involve feelings of sadness, grief and anger. After all, she has lost the love of her life, her best friend, even if it was an illusion, even if alcohol let her down in the long run.

If the members of her family have sought help for

themselves, if they are working on their own recovery, they may have a glimmer of understanding about the way she is feeling. Most families find it very difficult, even impossible, to understand what the recovering alcoholic is going through. She therefore needs the support of those who do understand – other alcoholics. No matter whether she decides to go for treatment or not, a professional experienced in dealing with addiction will advise her to seek the aid of Alcoholics Anonymous.

To the alcoholic woman

So, it is not enough to know you need help. It is not enough to know you need to stop drinking. You may already have been offered help and refused it. The first move is to accept help. This is vital. Unless you ask for help nothing can change. Trying to deal with alcoholism using only will-power is like trying to wish away a broken leg. No matter how much you wish you didn't have one, no matter how much you pretend it isn't there, no matter how much you try to carry on regardless, the leg remains broken. So it is with alcohol dependency.

Having recognised that you have alcohol dependency as a fact in your life, you need to learn to live with this fact. It isn't ever going to go away, no matter how much you ignore it. In order to have a better quality of life you need to surrender to this, accept this and look for help to undo the damage already incurred. Don't let false pride, shame or fear stop you from taking the opportunity to get well, to be happy.

Alcoholics Anonymous

Alcoholics Anonymous (A.A.) is a self-help organisation, a fellowship of alcoholics which has been flourishing since 1935. One night a man named Bill W, alone, shaken and frightened, decided that his only hope of staying sober was to try and help another alcoholic. Out of his meeting with Doctor Bob the next evening arose the miracle that is A.A.

More important than what was being said that evening was who was saying it. Instead of the usual refrain of 'This is what he should do,' Doctor Bob heard a recognisable voice say, 'This is what I did.' In listening to Bill W he helped not only himself but also Bill W. Together they supported each other to stay off drink. The story of course does not end there, and neither will yours.

At the first encounter with A.A. begins the end of the search for a place where you can find another human being with whom you can learn to be vulnerable, lose all pretence and defence, and trust that person not to hurt you because they are prepared to be vulnerable also. This may take a very long time. It is clear that it is very risky for you. After all if you have an alcohol dependency, you have not known how to cope with your feelings. You have tried to hide, even from yourself, by attempting to change your moods and medicate your feelings with alcohol.

Initially you will realise that you have been invited to share in the experience of recovery. Whatever you do, that invitation has been extended and remains. You have been invited to share as an equal. You have been offered understanding, equality and an already proven way out. You are made to feel that *you* are entitled to it; indeed you have earned it through your suffering.

The Twelve Step Programme

The First Step of A.A.'s Twelve Step Programme is 'We admit we are powerless over alcohol and that our lives had become unmanageable.' Powerlessness does not mean helplessness. So often in the past you have used this as an excuse for inappropriate or selfish behaviour, as an excuse to go on drinking. 'I didn't mean it'. 'I couldn't help it'. 'I didn't intend to'. You may have even blamed your alcoholism, laid the responsibility for your behaviour at the door of your addiction. Perhaps you blamed the drink itself. 'That wasn't really me. I was drunk'. 'It was the extra vodka that did it'. 'Whiskey does that to me'. 'Oh, it's the drink that does it'.

However, once the invitation has been extended to you by A.A., once you know about the A.A. Twelve Step Programme, you know about a way that works, that has worked for thousands of other alcoholics. In the early days of A.A. women members were a rarity. Today A.A. membership has indicated that one third of its members is female. A.A. discovered a secret that revolutionised the treatment of alcoholism — that the best person to help an alcoholic is another alcoholic who has discovered how to stay sober. To get A.A.'s help all you need is the wish to stop drinking. It doesn't matter who you are, what you've done, what age or sex you are, what social position you hold, whether you are a solicitor, a teacher, a doctor, a factory worker, a cleaner, a young mother at home with her children, a gardener or a nuclear physicist. A.A. isn't interested. They are only interested in helping you do something about your drink problem. You and every other member is anonymous. Nobody ever reveals who is a member. A.A. does not charge any fees. It doesn't have any boss. You are not expected to speak at a meeting, though if you want to, you can.

- It doesn't matter how or why you are alcoholic. Your alcoholism has taken on a powerful life of its own. Your recovery can only begin with a decision to stay away from the first drink. You are not to blame for your alcoholism. No one chooses addiction. You may have chosen alcohol, but you certainly did not want the baggage that came with it. As you became addicted, dependent on alcohol, so your life became unmanageable. The unmanageability of your life is the consequence of your powerlessness over alcohol. It is like picking up a stick. You cannot pick up one end without also picking up the other. Powerlessness is one end of the stick, unmanageability is the other. Insight into your alcoholism is not enough. Insight can only provide motivation; it cannot make you change. There are plenty of educated alcoholics sitting on barstools, drinking, who can pick out all the other alcoholics in the pub. Awareness must be followed by action.

Staying away from the first drink

No one can make the decision for you to stay away from the first drink. In A.A. you soon realise that even if you make that decision no one will force you to implement it. The choice begins and will always remain with you. You may not be responsible for your alcoholism, but you are responsible for your recovery. This is such an essential element in your recovery that the treatment centre in which I have worked commemorates it on one side of the medallion given to clients to celebrate their hard-won sobriety, with the words 'I am responsible'.

As you change your behaviour, your thoughts and attitudes, your feelings also change. As you admit to yourself that you are powerless over alcohol you begin to recognise that isolated incidents of control over your drinking were unimportant. What mattered was that when you had built up enough strength, or enough money, or enough credits with your family or workmates, then you drank again. You drank even when you didn't enjoy it, even when bad things happened. You drank despite all this. Your drinking isn't just a bad habit; you are powerlessness over alcohol. The problem isn't stopping drinking but staying stopped. Even though A.A. believes that the drinking is, in its own phase, 'The symptom of deeper troubles', they still leave you in no doubt that the first step is still the First Step. Recovery begins with 'staying away from the first drink'.

But stopping drinking is only the first step towards recovery. Recovery in A.A. is not so much to adopt new goals as to abandon old ones. If you attempt to hold on to old ideas, old opinions, beliefs and attitudes you will stay stuck and eventually drink again. It is not enough to just attend meetings, hoping something will 'rub off' on you. The real miracle occurs with your willingness to act, to change.

The physical aspects of alcoholism do not cause the suffering or damage that the progressive spiritual and emotional deterioration does. Every area of your life has become unmanageable. In recovery you need to address every area of your life in order to recover your losses. Remember also, an alcoholic is never cured. Chronic illnesses are only halted by death. Instead you need to work on arresting alcoholism's progress and heal the damage already inflicted on your body, mind and spirit.

When you stop drinking

When you stop drinking you may experience some psychological symptoms. You may crave drink; you may have mood swings and a whole range of unpleasant feelings. Fear and anxiety are common. Remember these will not last forever. You may become aware of aches and pains, but this is a sign that you are at last in touch with your own body rather than being numbed and anaesthetised. There may be restlessness and at the same time extreme fatigue. Your mind may be unable to concentrate, your body unable to relax, despite your tiredness.

Several nights of sleeplessness are common when you first stop drinking. Remember nobody dies from lack of sleep. You may have nightmares or disturbing dreams. This is because the brain may be catching up on dream time, alcohol having inhibited REM sleep, when dreaming occurs. It is important that you live through these initial feelings of discomfort, that you talk about what you are going through either to family and friends, at your A.A. meetings, or if you are lucky enough to be in treatment, to your group members and counsellors. Remember withdrawal symptoms are a sign of recovery. This is good news. Your body, mind and spirit are coming alive again. If you put your heart into recovery, you will only have to do it once. Say 'never again' and mean it. Now stop.

Remember to go for medical supervision of your detoxification. Abruptly stopping alcohol intake can be dangerous. Your doctor can help you with carefully monitored medication.

Stages of recovery

If you think that you cannot just stop, that you cannot give up drink, A.A. has a mental trick or plan to help you. Every alcoholic can give up drink for a day. You have probably done this in the past. So instead of putting your energies into worrying about next week, concentrate on not drinking today. Push tomorrow out of your head, and yesterday too. All you have to do is get through today without a drink, one-day-at-a-time. If the cravings are bad, break it down smaller. Just live one hour at a time, even ten minutes at a time. When the ten minutes are up, start the next ten minutes.

The higher power

The Second Step of A.A.'s Twelve Step Programme is 'Come to believe that a power greater than ourselves could restore us to sanity'.

In this step there is indeed the promise that you can recover and return to a healthy state of mind. This offers hope, hope of something better. When you drank, you drank hoping for something better. You drank to avoid loneliness, fear, sadness, shame, guilt, anger and unhappiness. But your drinking did not even lessen these feelings except perhaps temporarily. Once the alcohol was out of your system, the feelings were back, worse if anything.

The second step also declares that you are not a defective person, that you are not different from others. This may be one of your frightening beliefs, that maybe you are crazy, especially when you do something, yet again, that you promised you wouldn't. Faced with this illogical and irrational behaviour you may have wondered 'Am I mad?' Or maybe this was a peculiarly comforting thought: 'I must be crazy. Well, there's no hope for me then. I can do nothing about it. I'll have another drink.' The word to note here is *restore*, to bring back to sanity. This is not to say that examples of insane thinking don't continue even within sobriety: 'Perhaps I could have one, just one, more drink.'

The second part of this step talks about a higher power. The higher power is not defined. You are free to interpret this as you choose. After all, the Twelve Steps are not rules; rather they are reports of action taken, action which proved successful for other alcoholics. This acceptance of the alcoholic's ability to recover and the need for spiritual awareness is the second stage of action for recovery. A.A. is a spiritual programme. It is designed to help your spirit.

Alcoholism has harmed you physically, mentally and spiritually. It is no coincidence that one of the words most commonly used for alcohol is 'spirits'. This is how alcohol is used by alcoholics, to 'lift the spirit' or to fill that void in one's life, in one's soul. Alcohol becomes for them a false god. Forty years ago, before the advent of A.A., the psychiatrist Carl Jung told an alcoholic that there was hope for him if he could have a spiritual experience, a conversion experience. Carl Jung observed that unrecognised spiritual needs can lead people into great difficulty and distress. If alcohol use has been prompted at any level by spiritual thirst, the thirst will remain when the alcohol is removed. Part of recovery must be to quench that thirst.

A belief in God is not necessary for membership of A.A. You can give the word the meaning you choose. For some, a higher power is a personal god, or it may be the power of the group, or the philosophy of A.A. For others it is just something outside themselves. Whatever a higher power may mean to you, the second step reminds you that there is help out there.

Opening the door

The Third Step is 'Make a decision to turn our will and our lives over to the care of God as we understand Him [sic]'. A.A. says practising Step Three is like opening a door which to all appearances is securely locked. All that is needed is a key, and the decision to swing the door open.

A.A. tells us that there is only one key and it is called willingness.

Step Three on the path to recovery is about action; it is about accepting help. A.A. offers help (as do your counsellors and group members in a treatment programme). Are you prepared and willing to let them help you, to use their strength? When you go to A.A., listen to what is said; use the tips given; the recovering alcoholics know how they won. Most important of all is to get to the meetings. As many as you can. Two a day if you can. It doesn't matter if you don't know exactly what is happening or why you are there. You don't have to know exactly what you are going to get out of a meeting. Just being there is a statement of your commitment to yourself and a further acknowledgement of your powerlessness. You don't have to like it. You don't have to like the plaster cast you got on your broken leg. Even if it is uncomfortable, and awkward and strange at first, it can still give you your best chance, probably your only chance, at becoming happy and well.

Whether you attend a treatment programme or not, A.A. meetings are your lifeline. If you think you can't afford the time, remember the time you spent drinking. If you think you can't afford the expense, remember the money you spent on alcohol. If you think it is strange spending time in this way, remember the time you invested in getting to know your local pub or club. You may not know anyone at first, but after a few meetings you will. Take all the phone numbers you can get and use them. This is what fellowship is about. When you let others help you, they benefit too. As Bill W said, 'The best way to help an alcoholic is to let them help you.'

When people give you their phone number they do so in the expectation that you will phone them. You can phone them day or night, whenever you feel vulnerable, afraid or lonely. A.A. has a saying, 'Pick up the phone instead of picking up a drink.' The idea is to pick up a phone *before* you drink, not *after*.

It is a good idea to make a timetable of your meetings for the week. Don't leave it to chance. Schedule your life around the meetings rather than *vice-versa*. You won't always have to go to so many meetings; with time you will not be so vulnerable. For the first year of recovery it is essential that you put your meetings first. At the end of your first year you will be in a position to re-examine that commitment and decide what is best for your recovery.

Meanwhile you are not helpless. You are a strong individual who put her energy into maintaining her drinking. You were prepared to go to any lengths to get alcohol, to hide alcohol, to go on drinking. If you put one half of that energy and commitment into recovery you have it made. Anyone who thinks any woman is too weak, too stupid or too incapable of recovery only needs to step back and see how she conned, manipulated and manoeuvred her way to alcohol.

Stick with the 'winners'

Recovery means changing your life. It is truly a conversion process. This can be frightening or painful. Recovering alcoholics avoid pubs and drinking environments or drinking occasions. They avoid people who were only drinking companions rather than real friends. They spend time with other recovering alcoholics who have been sober for a period of time, the longer the better. They stick with the 'winners'.

Those people who don't understand your alcoholism need to be avoided in the early months of recovery, especially if they are likely to invite you to drink with them. Other well-meaning friends may try to reassure you that you are not really an alcoholic. It is better to avoid them at first. You can contact them later, when you are stronger. If you have several problems worrying you, your alcoholism problem needs to be made a priority. If there are marital problems, work problems, financial problems to be dealt with, realise that you cannot sort them out until you have got a handle on your alcohol dependency. Some matters may have to be sorted temporarily, as a holding measure. However, it is best not to make any important decisions or to start sorting out problem issues in the early days of recovery. The fact of the matter is that your thinking and emotions are still confused.

Taking care of yourself

Be good to yourself. Eat nice food; drink plenty of liquids. If you are a cigarette smoker, this is not the moment to cut back! You can stop smoking later, when you are less vulnerable and less likely to drink. The craving for drink is most likely to hit you when you are at your weakest. If you are hungry, angry, tired or lonely you are likely to want to drink. Therefore it is important to eat well, stay with supportive people, get the rest you need and deal with any anger that emerges for you. Talk about the anger, work out the tension by physical exercise, swimming, doing the ironing, playing tennis. Then talk about it some more. If you are fearful that you may revert to drinking, remember this is normal. A healthy fear of alcohol can help you to avoid it.

The time will come when you are tired or worried, nothing seems to be going right. The cat is missing. The baby is sick. The car won't start. The baby sitter has let you down. You can't relax. You need a drink. Don't do it. Remember that this too will pass. Everything will work out fine in the end, if you just don't drink.

This is your recovery. It is about discovering what works for you. It is not about learning to be the perfect wife, the perfect lover or the perfect mother. It is not about being the perfect anything. Nor is recovery about keeping others happy. It is about having freedom of choice. It is about not living your life conditionally with the limits and conditions set by alcohol. It is about being less preoccupied with drinking and plans for drinking. It is about being your own person, or learning how to be your own person.

Changing behaviour

The Third Step asks you to 'turn (your) life over to God'. By this is meant a change in behaviour. Turn is an action word. It is not just contemplation. Everyone has had the opportunity to do it their way. Your self-will has got you into severe problems. It is important to suspect your own feelings and thoughts. You cannot trust your own reactions because they may be setting you up to drink again. You therefore cannot trust your own will. You have turned your will over to another god, to alcohol. You believed it was a cure-all, an answer to everything, but it nearly destroyed you. Learning to trust again is part of the healing process involved in Step Three. Learn to trust others, to let them help you. You are not expected to give yourself into the control of God, rather into the 'care of God'. Alcoholics in recovery, while speaking about the spiritual aspect of the programme, describe it this way: 'Instead of finding a god which we can understand, we come to believe in a god who understands us.'

There is a story told about a woman who fell over a cliff. On the long fall down towards the ground she managed to grab hold of a shrub or branch growing precariously out of a crevice in the cliff face. Hanging there she began to pray, 'Oh dear God, please help me. Help me dear God, please help me!' From above she heard a comforting pleasant voice reply. The voice said, 'Let go, Trust me. Let go'. After a long hesitation she asked nervously, 'Is there anyone else up there?'

Sometimes a woman will try to white-knuckle her way through the early stages of recovery. She hangs on there, maintaining control and refusing to change anything. For her, recovery is a test of endurance. This makes life uncomfortable for all around her as she is resentful, angry and tense. However, doing it her way, is the way that kept her ill for years. Staying the way you are means staying stuck in a way of thinking and feeling where you need to drink.

Make yourself go to meetings. Make yourself listen.

Practise doing the little things that people suggest. Gradually you will learn the importance of being able to identify situations and your response to them that may constitute a danger to your sobriety. The important question is, 'What is happening for me now?' Long hours pondering past events, looking for answers to the question 'Why do I drink?' will not help unless you *explore* the why. This can be discerned from the present daily life events which propel you towards drink. Dealing with the now, the present, is very important. You have been avoiding your feelings, avoiding living in the present while you were drinking. If you are going to be happy as well as alcohol-free you will need to spend some time exploring your attitudes. This is at the heart of successful recovery. You are already changing how you think about alcohol. Because drinking alcoholically has affected the way you think and feel, these are areas you need to explore.

Alcoholism is an emotional disease. Drinking alcoholics have developed a range of rigid negative attitudes and feelings. They are often arrogant, full of stubborn pride, despite feeling bad about themselves. They are sensitive to criticism and full of self-pity, always thinking of themselves rather than of others. They may be intolerant and impatient, preferring to ignore unpleasant facts or situations. They are often angry and frightened people. They are also dishonest; lying to others and to themselves has become a way of life.

Uncomfortable, negative feelings such as loneliness, fear, anger and resentment are feelings on which you have drunk. You need to work on both your set attitudes and also the issues in your life which leave you feeling this way. Some of the healthy attitudes which can support you to remain sober are: accepting that life is not fair, allowing yourself to make mistakes, setting yourself realistic goals, stopping worrying or getting angry about things you cannot change, seeing things from other people's point of view, not expecting too much from others and not letting other people press your buttons. You need to work on replacing arrogance with humility, over-sensitivity with consideration for others, self-pity with gratitude, inability to stand frustration with patience, anger with caring, inability to face reality with acceptance, fear with trust and dishonesty with honesty.

All this may seem a tall order. This is where A.A. can help you. The Twelve Step Programme is a recovery programme developed over the years to help all recovering alcoholics regain self-respect, dignity, joy in living and emotional health. You can work on the A.A. programme within A.A. and also within any therapeutic support you may be obtaining: within one-to-one counselling with a therapist, with your sponsor in A.A., within your aftercare programme if you have received residential treatment. Many forms of therapy work side by side with your A.A. meetings to help you explore who you are, how you feel about important issues in your life and what you need to change.

Gaining self-knowledge

The Fourth Step of A.A. is 'Make a searching and fearless moral inventory of ourselves'. This step is about self-knowledge. When you are alcoholic you have strong feelings of guilt and shame because of the way you have been living. Perhaps these are feelings which were already present before you began drinking because of your life experiences. If you felt bad about yourself before, once you have been drinking alcoholically you will have a very poor regard for yourself. 'Worthless', 'A waste of space', and many other derogatory terms are used by alcoholic women about themselves.

These feelings of shame and low self-esteem nurture the alcoholism. It is easy to drink on these feelings, in an attempt to block them out. If you hold on to these negative beliefs about yourself, you are likely to drink again. Many alcoholic women are afraid to honestly look at themselves for fear they would discover that they really are horrible people. But it is only when you face and accept yourself for what you are that you gain freedom and confidence. It is only by accepting yourself and forgiving yourself your mistakes that you become free to hold your head up and look all other people in the eye with confidence and contentment.

It is important in recovery to stop denying who you are and what has happened to you in your life. You have drunk alcohol in an attempt to avoid many painful feelings about your life. In recovery you will learn to experience these feelings and to then move on and let go of them. You may require professional help to deal with some of the areas in your life. Treatment can help you acknowledge and enumerate those issues which are particularly difficult for you and which you may require professional guidance to deal with. Working on the Fourth Step with A.A. can also serve this purpose.

A.A. recommends that you write down your response to the Fourth Step. Guidelines for areas to examine are provided. This exercise helps you explore the whole of your experience, honestly and to the best of your ability, without omitting or censoring anything. It may not be perfect, but if it is your honest best it will open the door to many issues in your life. It recommends that you write about everything that happened to you and your reaction to it, without judgement or censure.

Through this inventory you have an opportunity to develop awareness of yourself, your feelings and your reactions. You will feel the pain of embarrassment, fear and guilt. Search out fearlessly all those events and things which fill you with uncomfortable feelings. Explore your personal weaknesses and character defects. Do not omit anything. If there is something you want to avoid or pass over, that is an uncomfortable area for you. It is something you may have drunk on. This inventory does not change things. It is a story of your feelings. As you explore those things you wince at or recoil from, remember these are not hurting anyone but you.

The Fourth Step helps you to explore how the past has

affected your world within. You are always ready to do the Fourth Step; it is the beginning of a lifelong process. It doesn't matter if you don't know how it works; you will know it works when you do it. If may be the first tangible evidence of your complete willingness to move forward. In it you focus on yourself, not on others. It helps you identify your strengths as well as your weaknesses, your gifts, your creativity and all your human qualities.

Moving beyond shame

The Fifth Step of the A.A. recovery programme is 'Admit to God, to ourselves and to another human being, the exact nature of our wrongs'.

In this step you address the issue of shame in your life and how it paralyses you and stops you from moving ahead in recovery. The belief that you are a bad person, that people would never accept or like you if they really knew you and what you have done in your life, is a crippling one. By involving yourself in A.A. and in treatment, by talking to others about your alcoholism, you are working on accepting and forgiving yourself.

As you allow yourself to feel guilt for what you have done and as you take responsibility for hurts inflicted, you can move on to decisive healing action. You can begin to make amends. You can begin to forgive yourself. It is important to share the exact nature of your wrongs, not vaguely or in general. Do not hold on to any issue, or any area that is causing you pain, shame or guilt. This will bring you back to drink. Relief only comes when you talk about things specifically. General words like terrible, horrible and bad just intensify your shame.

Choosing a sponsor

It is important to find the right person to talk to. Sharing everything with your husband or a family member is not a good idea; it may be too great a burden for them. Usually a counsellor, a cleric or your sponsor is the person chosen to hear your Fifth Step.

You need someone to get honest with, truly honest. A sponsor is an important person in your recovery. The idea is to find someone who is in a good committed recovery state for at least two years and who has been sober for that time. Normally you choose someone of the same sex. This is because your sponsor is someone to whom you will become very close. In order to avoid emotional confusion or sexual entanglements you are advised to pick a woman sponsor if you are a woman. If you are gay, then it is best to pick a sponsor of the opposite sex. When you look for a sponsor, look for someone who is working the programme. They may have a similar background to yourself, they may not. It will help if you pick someone you will like and get on well with but also someone whom you respect. You need someone who will challenge you, who will not be afraid to be honest with you. So choose someone you like and trust. Your sponsor will be someone who will get to know all about you, someone to whom you can safely talk about everything that is troubling you.

Living without alcohol can be difficult and it is important that there is someone to whom you can turn. Of course it is up to you to ask for the help you need. There is no point in having a sponsor when you don't see her or telephone her. If you cannot find the right sponsor or are unsure about one, you can always ask someone to be your sponsor temporarily.

Your Fourth and Fifth Steps encompass examination of such areas as character defects. These might include any or all of the following:

1. Self-centredness
2. Dishonest thinking
3. Pride
4. Resentment
5. Intolerance
6. Impatience
7. Envy
8. Phoniness

9. Procrastination
10. Self-pity
11. Touchiness
12. Fear
13. Perfectionism
14. Stubbornness/Rigidity

Your assets and abilities, your life history, your family or origins, those things you might feel guilty about, your relationships, your spirituality and your sexuality – these are some of the areas you are recommended to examine. Recovery is for the whole person.

Moving to change

The Sixth Step is 'Be entirely ready to have God remove all these defects of character'. This step calls for a commitment to change. There is a willingness to work on recovery, to let go of the drinking and the character defects, one day at a time. Rather than blaming the world, you take up the responsibility for changing your life, your actions and your attitudes.

In A.A. meetings all over the world, men and women testify that change is possible, that when they became willing to let go, to 'clean house' and ask their higher power to release them, their obsession to drink vanished. There is no point in waiting for your higher power to do this without *your* help. You must do your best, work to the limits of your ability. When you have gone as far as you can go, then your higher power, whatever that may be, will take over.

There is a story told about a young girl who wanted a bicycle. She went to her mother and asked her, pleaded with her, to know if there was any way she could get one. Because her mother loved her and because she knew how much her daughter wanted a bicycle, she told her that if she worked very hard and saved all her pennies, one day she might be able to buy one. The young girl was delighted and started straight away to save all her pocket money.

She also began to run errands and do chores to earn some extra cash.

A while later, she went again to her mother, showing her all the money which she had saved and asked when she could buy a bike. When her mother saw her longing she told her that they could go that day and look at the bicycles and see if she could afford one. The child was so excited she laughed and jumped the whole way to the shop. She saw a bicycle that was exactly what she wanted. When she looked at the price her face fell. Looking at her mother she said, 'No matter how hard I work, Mum, I will never be able to afford this bicycle, will I?' Kindly, her mother said, 'I'm afraid not. But I'll tell you what. If you give me everything you've got, I'll make up the difference and you can take the bicycle right now.'

So it is with recovery. You can change with the help of your higher power. You can overcome all your defects. The only question is 'Are you ready?' Open-mindedness is important here. The other side of the medallion given to the successful sober graduates of the treatment centre where I work says: 'Open to change'. This is a key step on the road to your recovery.

Understanding and acceptance

The Seventh Step is 'Humbly ask Him [sic] to remove our shortcomings'. Often your higher power will work through others, as you attend meetings, listen, apply the programme in your life and seek the wisdom of recovering addicts who are allowing the possibility of healing. People in the groups you attend support you as you change. Their hopeful and encouraging words, their understanding and acceptance, works a miracle in your life. As others love and care for you, you begin to see that you may indeed be worthwhile and lovable. You are being healed. Your attitude and outlook on life begins to change, your fear of people leaves you and you begin to know how to handle your life.

The story of the woman who wanted to visit heaven

and hell to see which she would prefer goes as follows: She presented herself at the pearly gates to St Peter. St Peter brought her first into a huge room with a long table in it stretching as far as the eye could see. In the room there was the most delicious aroma you could imagine. It was the smell of the tastiest soup ever cooked. The smell was so good that her mouth watered immediately. Sitting around the table were people with spoons in their hands. However, even though there were huge tureens of this delicious soup placed at intervals along the table, the people were emaciated and miserable looking. They were arguing and shouting at one another; the air was filled with hostility and tension. She could see that they were starving and full of anger and hate.

'This must be hell,' thought the woman. Without a word St Peter brought her into another room. It was exactly like the first, a huge room with a long table stretching into the distance. The aroma was the same. The woman ached with hunger. In this room, however, there was obvious conviviality, laughter and happy voices. Around the table sat well-fed, contented people. Each of them held a spoon in their hand.

'This must be heaven', thought the woman. 'But what is the difference? They both seem to have the same things.' Just then she noticed that those sitting around the table in the second room were using the long-handled spoons to ladle soup from the tureens in the centre of the table to feed each other. The striking aspect of it was they were feeding each other. The woman realised that this was the difference between heaven and hell. In hell the people had been self-centred, helping only themselves and not giving or accepting help from others. Because their spoons were so long, they could not feed themselves, so they were starving and unhappy. In heaven they gave help and received it. This story sums up the essence of A.A. and recovery.

Ending isolation

The Eighth Step is 'Make a list of all persons we have harmed, and become willing to make amends to them all'. This step deals with ending isolation. You may have been unaware when drinking of how you affected others. Indeed that detachment and isolation from others suited your drinking. You could deny that anyone else was harmed by your drinking. As you realise what it was like for the other people in your life, so you grow in empathy, in consideration and in care and concern for them.

It is important to add your own name to this list. You too have been affected by alcoholism. One of the most difficult tasks of recovery is learning to forgive and love yourself. Your drinking and consequent behaviour showed clearly that you have put little or no value on yourself. Each time you hurt someone or acted out your guilt feelings you were violating your own values. In time your feelings became numbed and suppressed to protect you from the shame and horror of how you were undermining your own dignity and self-respect.

You can make amends to yourself by recovering, by doing your best one day at a time. One sign that you are valuing yourself is how you treat your body. When women are drinking alcoholically they often neglect their health and their appearance. They don't eat properly and they sleep at irregular times of the day. Money goes on alcohol rather than on clothes. They may be bloated or obese because of their drinking, or because they have damaged their kidneys. Or they may have over-eaten. Many alcoholics drink coffee and smoke to excess.

By working on restoring your body to full health you can make amends to yourself for the damage inflicted by your drinking. You need proper food, rest and recreation. The mind and body are inter-related. If your body is unwell, you will probably start to feel depressed or over-anxious. Alcoholics frequently have difficulty relaxing in the first months of their recovery.

For years you may have sedated your body with

alcohol and perhaps with alcohol and tranquillisers. You have lost or never learned the ability to relax naturally. You may have a high level of anxiety. Rather than resorting to a glass of alcohol to cope with this physical tension, you need to learn how to relax. Exercise is a natural method of relaxation. Taking up a sport or an aerobic exercise like walking, jogging, swimming or cycling will help your body to relax. All exercise should be started gently and gradually. Giving yourself some time in the day just for yourself is important. This allows you space to unwind, relax and check-in with yourself. You need time to think, to be aware of your feelings, to be aware of your physical state. If you are a busy mother or have a career and perhaps the role of home-maker also, you may not take time even to be sick.

Setting aside some time every day to relax is essential. You could listen to soothing music, read a book, keep a journal, have a bath, go for a gentle stroll or just do some simple relaxation exercises. A relaxation class, or a meditation class, is a good idea if you want to improve your skills of relaxation. Stress is a danger zone for you anyway, because when you are stressed you are more vulnerable to cravings for alcohol. Stress is debilitating for everyone, but it is a particular hazard for you as a recovering alcoholic.

As a woman, your lifestyle probably involves playing several roles and having several jobs all at the same time. Today, women are without the support of the extended family network that they had in the past. Your outer appearance may have reflected your deteriorated emotional state. It is important in recovery to transform the outer as well as the inner. Though externals are not everything, a well-groomed appearance can add notches to your self-confidence.

It may take time for your body to get its gynaecological functions back to normal. Period pains often seem more severe when you stop drinking. This may be because you are used to being permanently sedated. Every pain seems worse at the start of recovery. See your doctor if you are worried. Giving yourself permission to look after your body by attending doctors and dentists is another way to develop self-worth.

Looking at the nature of your relationships, how you treated others, neglected them, used them, took advantage of them, helps you understand how you have hurt other people. You may have hurt them by not being there for them, by not offering love or support. You need to look at how you acted rather than holding on to resentment and blame. You cannot afford to let feelings of anger go unresolved and grow into resentment. Instead you need to express your anger in healthy ways and then let it go.

Restoring relationships

The Ninth Step is 'Make direct amends to such people whenever possible except when to do so would injure them or others'. This step in your recovery is about restoring relationships. Usually people will forgive you long before you forgive yourself. It is important to work on letting go of shame and guilt. By reaching out to them, by trying to make specific direct amends to them, you can ease their hurt as well as relieve your own feelings of shame.

When someone has hurt you there is usually a desire for that hurt to at least be acknowledged by the person who did it. Many of the consequences for your family may be such that you cannot make direct amends. You can never give back the time and love they have lost. The only amends you may have to offer are the acceptance of how you hurt them and your willingness to get well. For many, this is all, and more than, your family wants.

Sometimes family members are still hurting and they remain angry and distant. They may seem to reject your efforts at making amends. In this case all you can offer is your patience and understanding in dealing with their reactions and responses. Your family may be a source of concern for you in your recovery. Your family are usually the people you have hurt the most, the ones who have been on the receiving end of much of your alcoholic behaviour.

Alcoholism is very much a family illness in that all the family members become affected emotionally. Emotional attachment is the dynamic which holds a family together. Alcoholism attacks that very bond. When you are unavailable emotionally to your family, they have to find ways of coping with that rejection in order to survive. Some family members become angry with you, others will try to 'mind' you and protect you. Other family members may try to control you or they may just distance themselves either by physical distance (leaving home) or by emotional distance (becoming indifferent). Al-Anon is a fellowship which supports and encourages family members on their path to recovery.

Often family members see the alcoholic as the problem and resist the notion that they themselves may be part of the problem. They want the alcoholic fixed and are threatened by the notion that they may be affected at a deep emotional level and that it may take time for them to recover. It is a frightening thought for you, and for them, that their ability to relate to others and to deal with their feelings has become distorted by your drinking.

Many of the husbands of alcoholic women leave them. Research has indicated that nine out of ten husbands of alcoholic women will leave them compared to only one out of every ten women married to alcoholic men who leave their husbands (Survey published in September 1977 issue of *Good Housekeeping*). Even if your husband doesn't leave the home he may have totally divorced his life from yours, his emotions from the relationship.

If the family has joined Al-Anon, they will start to recognise the damage to themselves. They will be taking responsibility for getting on with their lives and their recovery, going to their appropriate fellowship and therapy groups. They will understand, to a degree, what is happening for the alcoholic. This is tremendous support for her. Families who refuse to go to Al-Anon may stay in almost total ignorance of the illness of alcohol dependency. As they did not understand the drinking, so they do not understand recovery.

If you are considering treatment, an important aspect to look for is a good family support programme, involving them in your treatment and inviting them to work on their own recovery. If members of your family don't trust you and are checking up on you or treating you as if you were still drinking, don't try to persuade or bully them into changing. Words won't help. They can't really hear. As you stay sober and change, they will start to see what recovery is about.

A sexual partner

Most partners are overjoyed when the alcoholic stops drinking. But some remain suspicious. Partners also sometimes feel very jealous because of A.A. They resent the time spent at meetings. Once again, if they attend Al-Anon they will begin to understand. If you have been attending a treatment centre there may be an aftercare group or other ongoing support for your partner's recovery. Sometimes relationships need more specific help, and marital therapy is required. Your sexual relationship may need time to become comfortable. Often you may be making love for the first time without any mood altering chemical in your system. Shyness and embarrassment is common. Your partner may not be enthusiastic about resuming a sexual relationship that has been damaged by your drinking. They may have been repulsed by the smell of alcohol, by your behaviour or actions. It may take time for desire, for trust and for intimacy to develop again. Sexual love is not just about intercourse or orgasm, it is also about kindness, consideration and emotional warmth. These are probably qualities which you lost through your drinking. Have patience. Try courting your partner again. Cuddling, comfort and warmth may be all that is appropriate at first.

As a woman alcoholic you may need to learn to be sexually assertive. You may need to learn how to make your needs clear, to be able to say 'no'. Frequently female alcoholics will abuse their own sexuality by using it as barter. Sex becomes a way of keeping a husband quiet, a system of credit to allay feelings of guilt because of drinking.

Your drinking may have served the purpose of putting an end to a sexual relationship. There may be abuse in the present relationship, or you may have been sexually abused as a child and have never addressed this issue. If there are sexual problems which continue into recovery, please do seek sex therapy. Counselling for any abuse suffered is essential.

Some relationships break up after recovery. The sad truth is that sometimes, consciously or unconsciously, a few people prefer their partner sick. Perhaps they no longer feel needed when she recovers, perhaps they do not feel able to handle an equal relationship. Sometimes relationships break up because the alcoholic woman realises that she has been avoiding dealing with difficulties for years by losing herself in the bottle. When she works on her recovery she may decide she needs to leave the relationship.

Sometimes when relationships do not get better it is because there is a second problem of alcohol or drug or gambling dependency.

The problems incurred by the children of alcoholics are often quite severe. Because they have had no experience of normal, happy relationships throughout their childhood they may find great difficulty in forming relationships of trust. For the adult children groups have developed to help them recover. These are known as ACOA groups (Adult Children of Alcoholics).

Maintaining personal growth

The Tenth Step is 'Continue to take personal inventory and when we are wrong, promptly admit it'. This is about maintaining growth in your recovery. It is important not to become complacent, to continue to take seriously the need to adjust the boundaries of acceptable/unacceptable behaviour. Unfortunately alcohol dependency is a relapsing illness. Arresting your illness comes through learning a whole new set of attitudes based on the Twelve Steps of the A.A. Programme. It is a conversion, a new way of life. Continued sobriety seems to depend on keeping these attitudes strongly reinforced by attendance at meetings and by exploration of your behaviour and feelings.

Relapses often occur when you begin to take sobriety for granted or when you simply get bored with A.A. and the initial enthusiasm goes stale. At that point you may drink 'because you are not willing to do everything necessary for you to stay sober'. You may have been able to convince yourself that you didn't need to do all the necessary things, and may not even realise that you were on the way to a relapse.

The frightening aspect of a relapse is that the person who relapses usually reaches the stage of drinking at which she stopped, immediately. She may even be drinking more. One explanation of the acceleration of the progression of the illness is that her guilt may be greater, due to greater insight, so therefore she has to drink more to wipe out the greater guilt. One way or another, women who relapse often pick up at the point they would have been at if they had never stopped drinking.

Relapse means a return to insanity. A relapse usually follows a period of irrational thinking. This could occur for a week, a month, even a year. Relapse support therapy can help an individual retrace the warning symptoms of the relapse. The progression is usually quite evident. Often the individual will have stopped attending meetings prior to drinking, but not always. The advice of phoning someone prior to drinking usually doesn't work because by that time it is too late. The time to prevent a relapse needs to be much earlier, at the start of the warning behaviour or attitude. Often your priorities become confused and your recovery has moved down the list, below work or recreation or a relationship. Complacency, believing that you are cured, or that you don't need to work so hard on your recovery, is another alarm signal.

When you relapse you may want to blame it on something or someone. The one factor that is usually common to all relapses is that the alcoholic was no longer working the Twelve Steps. If you are getting bored or disenchanted with A.A., ask yourself the following questions:

1. Do I have an anchor group, where I am known, where someone might recognise odd behaviour?
2. Am I in regular touch with my sponsor?
3. Am I working on the Twelve Steps?
4. What am I doing to help another suffering alcoholic?

These questions test your involvement in A.A. Not being regularly involved may be the first sign that you are setting yourself up to drink. A check-list of symptoms leading to relapse is used in A.A. These are sometimes called 'stinking thinking'. They include:

1. Exhaustion
2. Dishonesty
3. Impatience
4. Argumentativeness
5. Depression
6. Frustration
7. Self-pity
8. Cockiness
9. Complacency
10. Expecting too much from others
11. Letting up on discipline
12. Use of other mood altering chemicals like pills
13. Wanting too much
14. Forgetting gratitude
15. Thinking it cannot happen to me
16. Omnipotence

It is important to take a slip or relapse seriously. Tell someone about it; go to a meeting; contact your therapist/counsellor if you are in treatment. When you are accepted, understood and encouraged by your group members, this will help lessen the likelihood of another slip/relapse. Shame and discouragement is much more likely to cause a relapse than is understanding and support.

Seeking further intimacy

The Eleventh Step is 'Seek through prayer and meditation to improve our conscious contact with God as we understood Him [sic], praying only for knowledge of His [sic] will for us and the power to carry that out'. This step in your recovery is about your intimacy with God or with your higher power. It is your responsibility to define your own spirituality. When drinking you may have been angry with God for leaving you to suffer. In recovery the development of a trust in an understanding, loving God may be difficult. First you need to learn how to pray, how to talk to God just as you talk to your other friends.

Showing gratitude for the blessings you now enjoy is one way you can increase your contact with your higher power. Rather than asking for material things, A.A. prompts you to ask for wisdom, strength, insight, courage and guidance. Just as we need to exercise our body for bodily strength, so we need to exercise our spirituality for spiritual strength. You can encourage this by setting aside time to be alone, time to listen. Seek out places and situations that encourage you to be quiet and receptive. Allow time to be calm. Become free to listen and to learn.

Giving as its own reward

The Twelfth Step is about giving as its own reward. 'Having had a spiritual awakening as the result of these steps, we try to carry this message to alcoholics, and to practise these principles in all our affairs'.

The joy of life, of living, is the theme for this step. It is talking about love which has no price tag. There is safety and security in this. When you receive a great gift, when you experience enjoyment or pleasure, a natural human reaction is to want to share it. Even when you read a good book, you tell your friend. When you have experienced the joy and contentment of sobriety you will want to carry the message to others, not to convert or save, but as an expression of that which you have received. Your living example of how the programme works will pass a message of joy and hope on to the next alcoholic.

Recommended reading

Understanding alcoholism

Kinney and Leaton, (1983) *Losing the Grip*, Mosby, London.
Maxwell, R., (1987) *The Booze Battle*, Ballintine, London.

Treatment of addiction

A.A. World Service Inc., (1976), *Alcoholics Anonymous: The Big Book*, Third edition.
Anderson, A. J., (1981), *Perspectives on Treatment*, Hazelden, New York.

Drug dependency

Mc Auliffe, R.M. and Mc Auliffe, M.B., (1975) *The Essentials of Chemical Dependency*, American Chemical Dependency Society, Minneapolis.
Ditzler, J.J. and Haddon, C., (1986) *Coming Off Drugs*, Papermac, London.
Neild, L., (1990), *Escape from Tranquillisers and Sleeping Pills*, Ebury Press, London.

Family issues

Beattie, M., (1989), *Beyond Co-dependency*, Hazelden, New York.
Beattie, M., (1990), *Co-dependent No More*, Hazelden, New York.
Hope and Recovery, a Twelve step guide for healing from compulsive sexual behaviour, (1987), Compcare, Minneapolis.

Directories

Directory of Alcohol, Drugs and Related Services (in the Republic of Ireland), Golden Pages.
Directory of Organisations Concerned with Substance Abuse, An Roinn Sláinte (Department Of Health)
Guide to Counselling Therapy, the Irish Association for Counselling Directory, (1991), Wolfhound Press, Dublin.

Addresses

Ireland (south)

The Health Promotion Unit
Department of Health,
Hawkins House,
Hawkins Street,
Dublin 2
Tel: (01) 6714711

Alcoholics Anonymous
109 South Circular Road
Dublin 8
Tel: (01) 538998/537677
Answering Service (6-10 pm)
01 6795967

Cork: Answering Service
(8.30-10.30am) 021 500 481

Limerick: Answering service
Tel: (061) 311222

Hospital Services, Advisory
and Counselling Services
Republic of Ireland
*See Directory of alcohol, drugs
and related services (Golden
Pages)*

Alcohol Treatment Unit
Baggot St. Community
Hospital,
18 Upper Baggot Street,
Dublin 2.
Tel: (01) 6607838

Cluain Mhuire Service
Newtownpark Avenue,
Blackrock,
Co Dublin.
Tel: (01) 2833766

Community Addiction
Counselling
Health Centre
Main St., Tallaght,
Dublin 24.
Tel: (01) 515397/515764

The Marley Centre
The Mews, Eblana Ave.,
Dun Laoghaire,
County Dublin.
Tel:(01) 280 7269/280 9795

Rutland Centre Ltd
Knocklyon Rd.,
Templeogue, Dublin 16.
Tel: (01)
946358/946761/946972

St John of God Hospital,
Stillorgan, Co Dublin.
Tel: (01) 288 1781

St Patrick's Hospital,
Steevens Lane,
James's St.,
Dublin 8.
Tel: (01) 6775423

Stanhope Alcoholism
Treatment Centre
Lr. Grangegorman,
Dublin 7.
Tel: (01) 6773965

Alcohol and Drug Counselling
Services.
1 Coote Tce.,
Portlaoise, Co Laois.
Tel: (0502) 21634 Ext 409.

St Loman's Hospital,
Mullingar,
Co Westmeath.
Tel: (044) 40191

Alcoholism Counselling
Service,
St Brigid's Hospital,
Ardee, Co Louth.
Tel: (041) 53264.

St Conal's,
Letterkenny,
Co Donegal.
Tel: (074) 21022

Aiseiri,
Roxvorough, Wexford.
Tel: (053) 41818

Alcohol and Drug Abuse
Treatment Centre,
Arbour House,
Douglas Road, Cork.
Tel: (021) 968933.

Alcoholism Counselling
Service,
Merlin Park Hospital,
Galway.
Tel: (091) 53595.

Alcoholism Counselling
Service,
St Mary's Hospital,
Castlebar, Co Mayo.
Tel: (094) 21733.

Ireland (north)
Northern Ireland Council for
Voluntary Action
127 Ormeau Road,
Belfast. BT7 1S
Tel: (0232) 321224

Central Office of A.A.
152 Lisburn Road,
Belfast BT9 6AJ
Tel: (0232) 681084 (office hours)

Northern Ireland Regional
Unit,
Shaftesbury Square Hospital,
116-122 Great Victoria St.,
Belfast BT2 7B6.
Tel: (0232) 329808

Britain

The Standing Conference on
Drug Abuse (SCODA)
1-4 Hatton Place
Hatton Garden
London EC IN 8ND
Tel: (071) 430 2341

Scottish Drugs Forum
5 Oswald Street
Glasgow 61 4 QR
Tel: (041) 221 1175

Welsh Committee on Drug
Misuse Secretariat
c/o HSSPIA
Welsh Office
Cathays Park
Cardiff CF1 3NQ
Tel: (0222) 823 925

Alcoholics Anonymous
PO Box 514
11 Radcliffe Gardens
London SW10 9B6.
Tel:(071) 352 9779

Council for Involuntary
Tranquilliser Problems
Cavendish House
Brighton Road
Liverpool L22 5N6.
Tel: (051) 525 2777

Alcohol Concern,
305 Gray's Inn Rd.,
London WCIX 8QF.

Addiction Treatment Centre
Queen Mary's University
Hospital,
Roehampton Lane,
London SW15 5PN
Tel: (081) 789 6611,
Ext. 2309.

District Addictions Service,
39 Abbey Rd.,
Torquay,
Devon TQ2 5NQ.

Alcohol and Drug Counselling
Service,
Portland House,
3 Portland Street,
Lincoln.
Tel: (0522) 521908

Scottish Council on Alcohol,
137-145 Sauciehall St.,
Glasgow G2 3EW.

Townhead Addiction Centre,
45 Townhead,
Irvine KA12 OBH.
Tel: (0294) 5631

Drug and Alcohol Project,
99 Rowan Street,
Blackburn,
Bathgate EH47 7ED.
Tel: (0506) 634898

For a full catalogue of
Attic Press *titles*
please write to:

Attic Press
4 Upper Mount Street
Dublin 2.
Ireland.
Tel: (01) 661 6128
Fax: (01) 661 6176